D0273827

CYBER SECURITY BASICS

Protect your organization by applying the fundamentals

DON FRANKE

Copyright © 2016-2018
by Don Franke

First printed, January 2016

This book is dedicated to my family, without whose patience and support this book would not have been possible.

CONTENTS

SECTION ZERO: BACK TO BASICS

You can't build a great building on a weak foundation. You must have a solid foundation if you're going to have a strong superstructure.

Gordon B. Hinckley

One of the worst man-made disasters in history is the collapse of a coliseum in Fidenae, Italy in the year 27 A.D. This catastrophe resulted in the death of over 20,000 people. To prevent tragedies like this from ever occurring again, the Roman senate passed laws that mandated that all large stadiums be built on a "sound foundation." This event provided the world with a valuable learning lesson that has influenced building construction ever since. [1]

A building with a solid foundation rarely falls on its own. It can even prove itself resilient against significant attacks. The same goes for a security program that is built and reinforced using sound design principles and best practices. This book is intended as a guide for identifying and implementing solutions that support a solid information security program. This could be a program that does not yet exist, or one that is being improved (and there will always be room for improvement.) Security solutions and programs cannot be set in stone, which is one thing that separates the foundation of a security program from physical structures.

This book is not meant to be a comprehensive text on every aspect of information security. Instead, the goal is to cover the fundamentals. Organizations can establish a competent and effective information security program by focusing on best practices, which translate into specific security controls and processes to support them. The goal of this book is to help reduce the technical hurdles that sometimes prevent solutions from being implemented. This may be due to a lack of understanding or feeling overwhelmed by the myriad choices that are available. Too much complexity is a deterrent to security (a concept that is covered in more detail later in this section.) The objective is to clear some of the technical fog that often surrounds and impedes information security efforts from being successful.

For this book, an organization or entity can be defined as one of the following:

- A for-profit company
- A non-for-profit organization or foundation
- A federal or local government unit
- A library, hospital, or school

Just as the size and composition of an organization can vary, so can the makeup of the team responsible for maintaining the security of its information assets. The organization may be fortunate enough to have a dedicated InfoSec or cyber security team with an appropriate level of staffing. Or it may be just a single individual who performs these duties while juggling several other responsibilities. Regardless of the size of the team, the experience level of those on the team, or size or scope of the organization, this book will hopefully provide the fundamentals for building a new, or reinforcing an existing, information security foundation.

0.1 BUILDING A FOUNDATION

This book is intended to provide an InfoSec primer for those with a beginner to intermediate skill level in the field. Hopefully this book will also provide value to those who are experienced with the challenges of protecting an entity's data, network, endpoints and employees from cyber-attacks. The goal is to demystify some of what may be the more complicated technical aspects of InfoSec, and to provide the fundamentals of a good information security program that can be executed by individuals of all skill and experience levels.

Ostensibly everyone at an organization is playing on the same team (not including the insider threat.) So, there is no reason why security controls cannot be implemented in a way that is conducive and minimally disruptive to IT operations, while protecting against attacks that originate from both inside and outside of the organization.

0.2 DEMYSTIFYING IT SECURITY

By demystifying IT security, the chasm that separates security and non- security groups can be bridged so that everyone can work together to raise the security posture of the organization. Focusing on clear, easy to understand best practices can clear the fog that obscures many security concepts.

The contents of this book are broken up into the following three main sections of information security:

- Protect: Take steps to implement controls to prevent attacks and protect the organization.
- Detect: Implement sensors and monitoring solutions that alert appropriate personnel when certain security events or incidents take place.
- Respond: React to security events and incidents quickly and appropriately.

Technical details should not get in the way of practicing good security. Security does not need to be overly complicated. If best practices are followed, most security weaknesses can be mitigated, and most attacks we read about in the news almost every day could be prevented.

0.3 USING A RISK BASED APPROACH

A risk-based approach may be the best way to provide some clarity. Focus first on the risks to the organization. Once you identify a list of risks, this list can be prioritized according to severity, which helps identify what to focus on first. Some questions to ask during the risk gathering process include:

- What are the biggest threats?
- What does the organization value most?
- What kind of attack would be the most damaging to the organization?

By taking the time to answer these questions, you can focus the finite resources that are available on the highest priority items first. But remember: if everything is a priority then nothing is a priority. There is a concept called the defender's dilemma. The gist of this term of art is that the defender has to protect all points of a system, yet an attacker only has to find one exploitable weakness to be successful. Since not all possible points of attack can be completely protected, risk management can help determine the most important points that need to be defended. Due to resource constraints, it is nearly impossible to fortify every aspect of an organization. Therefore, a better approach is to approximate and apply controls to areas where the most benefit can be achieved. Another concept to be aware of is residual risk. When security controls are applied, risk is reduced. The risk that remains after applying these controls is the risk that is left over, or residual risk. You should continually work on reducing residual risk.

0.4 GENERAL SECURITY CONCEPTS

Each security decision that is made should address at least one of the following concepts in this section. If it doesn't, challenge its value. Implementing a new control means making a change to the production environment, and any change runs the risk of breaking something that was working before, or of even increasing the attack surface. Changes should not be taken lightly. Any change that is made should maintain, if not improve, the security posture of an organization. Therefore, if you do decide to implement a security control, the net benefit of that change should be able to be mapped back to a core security concept.

Speaking of change for change's sake, Security Theater is one of my favorite expressions. It basically means implementing a security control only for the sake of saying that a security control has been implemented. It's just busy work, in other words, providing no actual improvement in security. It can actually make things worse! Since changes of this type do not make the organization any safer, Security Theater is something to avoid.

Changes also run the risk of increasing complexity. There is the rule that the more complex something is, the greater the chance that something will to go wrong with it. In a security context, complexity increases the chance of vulnerabilities and bugs that can be exploited. In addition to value, proposed changes should also be evaluated based on the added complexity they bring. Changes that increase complexity should be considered carefully, as they can adversely impact the overall security of the organization.

The following can be considered the top 10 principles that security professionals should follow, in no particular order.

0.4.1 LEAST PRIVILEGE

Objects can be protected by limiting access to them. Permissions, otherwise known as privileges or rights, can be assigned to objects. An object can be a protected resource like a document, a database, a system, etc. Restricting how a subject can interact with an object is an example of hardening. Hardening is applying security best practices to an object to make it more resilient to attacks.

Access permissions can be enforced and managed by using an access control solution. By following the principle of least privilege, permissions are explicitly defined based on the rights that a subject requires on an object. Permissions assigned to objects do not exceed what is necessary. Least privilege is also known as "need to know."

To effectively manage access for all subjects and objects, a ticket system can be utilized so that permission changes get the appropriate approvals and are documented. Ideally, access is tied to Human Resources so that permissions are based on the role of the employee, and that those same permissions are revoked if that employee separates (e.g. quits, gets fired, etc.) from the organization.

A permissions snowball is a phenomenon where the amount of access someone has directly reflects of the amount of time he or she has been with the organization. Privileges are continually granted to the user as that person changes roles, but they are never revoked. This is due to poor access management processes. Effective access management can help ensure that users only have the permissions needed to perform the job, and no more. When someone changes roles, access rights for the previous role should be revoked, and the rights needed for the new role should be granted.

0.4.2 SEPARATION OF DUTIES

To protect against the insider threat, permissions should be designed such that there is no single individual with access to everything. Excessive privileges can give individuals of questionable morals the opportunity to commit end-to-end fraud. The protection against this is to create logical barriers between systems and functionality in the form of a secure permissions design.

Separation of duties is like the principle of least privilege, except the separation of duties is more focused on distributing permissions among more than one individual. For example, let's look at the IT systems of an insurance company. To reduce the chance of fraud being committed by an employee, separation of duties should be used to prevent the same person from being able to both create a new insurance policy, and then file a claim against that policy. If one person were able to do both actions, insurance fraud could be the result.

When designing a new system, or hardening an existing one, analysis should be done to determine what permissions subjects should have on objects. This analysis should include playing out different negative scenarios where insider fraud can be committed. These scenarios can then be used to identify permissions, access controls, and the roles individuals will serve. Once the controls that have been identified are implemented, the chance of insider fraud can be greatly reduced.

0.4.3 CONFIDENTIALITY

Even in the world of social networks and general acceptance that "privacy is dead", there is still some data that needs to remain confidential. This need could be driven by regulatory or legal requirements, as well as to prevent costly data breaches. Ensuring the confidentiality of sensitive data means limiting access to these data assets to only authorized individuals.

The following steps are part of a process that can be used to identify data that should be treated as confidential:

- Identify all the data that the organization uses and retains. The result of this exercise should be a data inventory or data dictionary.
- Understand what regulations and legal requirements the organization needs to adhere to. These requirements should include how confidential data should be defined. There may also be an organizational policy regarding data and data retention. If so, these policies should also be consulted to determine how to correctly define confidential data.
- Review the organization's data inventory (e.g. customer name, mailing address, etc.) and assign a confidentiality label to each data item. The labeling should follow the confidentiality labels recommended by relevant regulations and policies.

Take the time to identify all the data that will be transmitted and stored. All data that is used by production networks and systems should be covered. To be thorough, though, include development and test environments as well. A data classification exercise is worth the effort. By identifying the confidentiality requirements of data, the appropriate controls, processes, and architectural design can be implemented. A solution such as encryption for data in transit and at rest is one of the best ways to ensure that this security principle is followed. Encryption by itself is not a solution however; it also needs to be implemented properly.

0.4.4 INTEGRITY

Maintaining the integrity of data, systems and software means ensuring that those objects have not been subjected to unauthorized changes. These can be changes that are done either intentionally or accidentally.

System files are an excellent example of objects whose integrity is critical to protect. Changes to these files could be the result of actions performed by an adversary in the form of malware that has infected a system. These integrity checks can be performed by an agent installed on a device, by the operating system (OS), or by the low-level BIOS that underlies and supports it all. As integrity controls may be available in different areas of a device, be familiar with all the options available to help make the right decision about how best to prevent unauthorized changes from being made on critical files.

Documents and databases can also have integrity requirements. There are some files that should never be changed once they are created, such as log files. Using integrity checks on log files will let the appropriate teams know if modifications have been made or attempted. Detection of a user or process making changes to a log file could lead to the discovery of a malicious actor trying to cover his or her tracks.

0.4.5 KEEP IT SIMPLE

Complexity is bad for security. They say the devil is in the details, and indeed it is in the obscure, less-understood dark corners of code and networks that opportunity presents itself to attackers. The more complicated something is (such as application code, network design, or firewall rules), the greater the chance there is something wrong with it. These flaws could be security vulnerabilities.

The Keep it Simple, Sir (KISS) approach should be used whenever possible when implementing IT and security-related solutions. This principle is also known as economy of mechanism. [2] Less complexity results in software and systems that are easier to use and support. It also makes it easier to find vulnerabilities and fix them. And when problems do arise, a less-complex system will be easier to troubleshoot to find the root cause.

Information systems and security are complicated enough. When deciding which solutions to use, and how they should be implemented, the KISS principle should be kept in mind. If a proposed change seems to introduce more complexity but not much value, it should be reconsidered.

0.4.6 LOGGING

Logging is the recording of activities performed by individuals and IT assets. For each event that is logged, the following table lists the properties that should, at a minimum, be recorded.

Term	Definition
Who	Source of the action: user, system, or process
What	Description of the action taken
When	When the event took place: a timestamp that is synchronized across systems.
Where	Object involved or acted on to perform action

Table 0.1: Each log event should tell "who did what, when and how."

Logging gives an organization the ability to monitor the actions of employees, systems and software. It can also provide valuable insight that can be used to research activities, such as security events that can turn out to be security incidents. The current news regularly provides examples of successful attacks that include a prolonged presence on a network. This means malware and other compromises ran undetected. Ensuring that systems perform effective logging and capturing those events in a centralized log repository that is actively monitored, is key to detecting malicious activity like this.

The quality and integrity of the log data needs to be unquestionable. Security events and incidents should be responded to with the assumption that any log files that are involved will later be used as evidence for investigatory and legal proceedings. If there is any doubt that the log data has not been tampered with, that data may become inadmissible as evidence. As a result, preservation of the log data should follow a formal chain of custody process. Best practices for effective logging and log data preservation is covered in a later section.

0.4.7 DEFENSE IN DEPTH

A castle provides a good example of using a defense in depth security strategy. A castle does not rely on a single defensive measure to provide total protection for the kingdom within. Some of these defenses include:

- Building the structure in a mountainous or hilly region that provides a high vantage point so that adversaries can be seen from afar
- A moat with a single drawbridge that can be retracted at the time of attack
- An outer wall
- An inner wall
- A main gate that provides a chokepoint

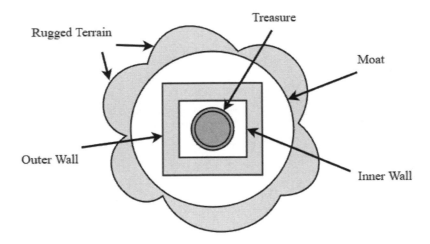

Figure 0.1: Castles and other fortifications often used a defense in depth strategy.

Fast forward to today. When it comes to IT systems, a single solution or control should never be relied on to provide total protection for an organization.

Figure 0.2: Most of today's networks are protected by following a defense in depth approach.

The use of layered security can help ensure that an organization is still protected even if a single control fails. As in Figure 0.1, if the attacker gets past the firewall, the attack will hopefully be stopped by a subsequent security control. This is analogous to a castle where, if the enemy breaches the outer wall, there is still the inner wall and several other defenses to contend with.

An adversary will follow the path of least resistance to reach a goal. If security controls are in place that block all attempts, the attacker will seek an alternate route. Or a different target altogether. A well- defended fortress not only can defend itself against attacking hordes, but also deter enemies from expending the resources required to acquire any treasures protected within its high walls.

0.4.8 FAIL SECURELY

All software has bugs. Just like people, there exists no software that is perfect. Regardless of how pristine the software appears, it is just a matter of time before a security vulnerability is discovered. It could be code that is written by in-house or contracted developers, software that runs in vendor-provided solutions such as a security appliance, or components that developers download from open source repositories over the Internet.

Sometimes the issues are discovered accidentally. Other times it is the vendor or development community that finds (and hopefully fixes) them. But there may also times be when it is an adversary who finds the vulnerabilities, and perhaps keeps this information confidential, or sells it to the highest bidder.

The methods by which software vulnerabilities are found can also vary. Sometimes it is by accident through non-malicious usage or a review of the software. Other times it can be the result of someone intentionally attempting to break the software in order to see what happens. When intentionally causing an application or server to fail, the attacker can gain information that can be used in a subsequent attack. This is a form of reconnaissance. Software failures can also present an opportunity for the adversary, such as privilege escalation or authentication bypass.

Software that is not designed to fail safe or fail secure has an increased chance of providing opportunities to an attacker. When software crashes, it should handle the failure in a safe and secure way. A secure software design will help ensure this. Some examples of the actions that software should take when encountering an exception, error or failure include:

- Close all connections to databases and protected resources
- Clear out all sensitive information from memory and caches
- Terminate sessions and invalidate tokens

Examples of information that can be provided by software that does not follow the fail secure principle include:

- Database connection information
- Authentication credentials
- Directory information and drive mappings
- Technical details about the software and systems it is running on

Software should be developed and implemented under the assumption that it will crash at some point. This crash should not provide an opportunity for attackers. The "fail safe" principle, where all possible exceptions and errors are handled in a consistent and secure way, should be part of the design to prevent sensitive information disclosure and other kinds of attacks.

0.4.9 COMPLETE MEDIATION

Complete mediation supports the "trust but verify" principle. Many applications use protected resources like databases, file shares, authentication servers, etc. When software interacts with these types of resources, the design of the software should ensure that this interaction takes place in a circumspect way. For example, software should not open a connection to a database and leave that connection open for the duration of the user session. This is like opening the door for a guest, then leaving it open for the rest of the day. While it was opened only for a specific purpose, the persisted open connection presents a potential opportunity for the adversary to gain access to sensitive data and files.

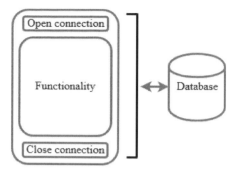

Figure 0.3: When a large block of functionality uses a single open connection, this presents a window of opportunity for an adversary.

By following the principle of complete mediation, access to protected resources is validated before it is provided. This validation occurs every time access is requested. Once the use of the resource is complete and no longer needed (such as a data fetch from a database) the connection is immediately closed.

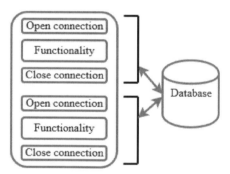

Figure 0.4: Explicitly requesting access before using it, then immediately terminating that access when it is no longer needed, severely reduces windows of opportunity for an attacker to leverage.

Code sections (a.k.a. the functionality) that use a database connection are surrounded by their own separate "open connection" and "close connection" blocks. An access validation check is performed in the open connection blocks, and the access termination is performed in the close connection blocks. By following the principle of complete mediation, an adversary has a severely reduced chance of having access to open connections to protected resources.

0.4.10 OBSCURITY IS NOT SECURITY

The design itself is what provides the security, not the secrecy of the design. Industry-accepted encryption standards are a good example of open design. The details about how these encryption algorithms work is publicly available. Despite this, they can provide best in class security when implemented correctly. Even though obscurity itself should not be considered a complete solution, a security strategy should include making the job of the attacker as difficult as possible. The cost of obtaining the objective should exceed its value. Information can be hidden strategically, such as making web server information non-obvious to scans.

```
HTTP/1.1 200
Server:  Apache/2.4.10 (Unix)
Date:  Sun, 06 Dec 2015 21:12:26 GMT
Content-Type:  text/html
Content-Length:  166
Connection:  close
```

Figure 0.5: Some publicly-available information can be useful to attackers, such as web server banners, which could provide clues as to what vulnerabilities the server may have.

Some ways to hide or disguise Internet-facing web servers include:

- Hiding HTTP header information
- Changing banner information
- Disabling unnecessary services like ICMP (ping)

Information can not only be hidden from plain view but can also be deliberately changed. Disguising or changing information to throw off the adversary is also known as counterintelligence or dis-information. Also, air-gapping (removing Internet access) may help protect information from being easily accessible. Security should be regularly evaluated and can be done in the form of penetration tests, otherwise known as red team assessments. These can reveal what information about the organization can be easily obtained and identify hardening opportunities that should be taken.

Operating under the assumption that certain information will never be discovered is a setup for failure. The focus should be on making and implementing the best security choices, not on hoping that certain information will never be discovered.

0.5 SECURITY MATURITY LEVELS

Many of the topics in the following sections have a level indicator. This indicator represents the level of maturity and expertise that a security team should have to effectively deploy the respective security control. It does not necessarily represent the value the control can bring to an organization. However, this indicator will hopefully assist the reader to identify and prioritize the most appropriate security solutions and controls.

For an organization that is just starting to implement an information security program, Level 1 items may be the place to start. For those organizations that already have an InfoSec program that is more mature and established, Level 2 or 3 objectives may be more appropriate. These levels are included in sections one and two of this book.

These maturity levels are not meant to indicate their importance or effectiveness. They are meant to offer suggestions for a phased and iterative approach to build and constantly improve an information security program.

These recommendations are based on my experience. The intent is to help the reader focus on implementing best practices first, which provides a solid foundation on which to build.

0.5.1 LEVEL 1

A security best practice, core to the foundation of any IT security program. Intended for a newly created security team, or an individual recently tasked with improving the IT security of an organization. This could be starting with a blank slate, or with some basic security controls that are already (or at least partially) implemented.

0.5.2 LEVEL 2

Controls to consider once the organizational security program has a solid foundation of controls and processes and is effective at providing security. Intended for an established security team or operations center that has been functioning for some time, with repeatable and effective processes and controls in place.

0.5.3 LEVEL 3

Solutions that improve visibility and fill the gaps between the controls and processes utilized by an effective information security program. Intended for a security team or Security Operations Center (SOC) that has repeatable and effective security processes that have proven themselves in the form of detecting and stopping attacks. They have perhaps even experienced "trials by fire" by responding to security incidents. There is enough staff, resources, and support from leadership to push the security program to "best of class" status by implementing controls in every security category and working towards a state where every aspect of the network and endpoints are actively monitored and effectively protected.

0.6 SUMMARY

Each decision made about controls and processes should be able to be mapped to one or more of the security principles discussed in this section. If it doesn't, reconsider whether the effort will actually improve the security of the organization, as it may just result in Security Theater. An increase in complexity has a potentially adverse impact on the security of an organization's network, systems and software. Finally, as you read on, consider the maturity levels assigned to the security controls that are discussed. These security maturity levels are intended to serve as a guide to help determine which controls are appropriate for your own organization's information security program.

Is this book comprehensive? No. Is there a lot about cyber security that won't be included? Absolutely. My goal here is to help those who are just starting, or those who are looking for inspiration about where to go next. It will hopefully provide something that promotes further reading and investigation into the different aspects of cyber security, of which there are plenty.

Overall, I think Bret Arsenault, Chief Information Security Officer of Microsoft, summed it up well when he said the following: "I firmly believe that security is a journey and not a destination. It's also an issue that must be addressed holistically by the industry and not by a single vendor. It's only by working closely with our partners, the security ecosystem and governments around the world, that we can ensure consumers and businesses are able to trust the technology they use and don't view security as a barrier to technology adoption." [3]

0.7 TERMS AND DEFINITIONS

The following are terms discussed in this section with their definition.

Term	Definition
Asset	Something of value to an organization, that therefore requires protection.
BIOS	Basic Input Output System. The low-level software that allows a computing device to boot up by managing its hardware components such as memory, display, and audio. If the BIOS gets compromised, it should be assumed that the operating system and all applications running on the device are also compromised.
Chain of Custody	A process that is followed to demonstrate that data has not been tampered with since its creation. This is critical for preserving data that may later be used in legal investigations and proceedings.
Complete Mediation	Verifying the permission to a protected resource before providing access to it, every time.
Confidentiality	Ensuring that sensitive information is accessible only by authorized individuals.
Counterintelligence	Disguising or deliberately changing information to throw off the attacker.
Defender's Dilemma	A defender must protect all points all the time, while an adversary often just has to find one vulnerability to be successful.

Defense in Depth	Not relying on a single control to provide all security.
Economy of Mechanism	Reusing existing components versus creating components from scratch. This helps ensure that the design and implementation are as simple as possible, since complexity increases the chance of vulnerabilities. Economy relates to cost in terms of lines of code or unique components used. Also see the KISS principle.
Fail Safe	Also known as "fail secure." When an application or system encounters an exception, the design of the application or system should ensure that the failure happens in a secure way. Proper exception handling can include closing connections to protected resources, not divulging sensitive or excessive information, and not providing elevated access.
Fail Secure	See Fail Safe.
Hardening	Improving the security of an object by taking actions such as restricting permissions or removing unnecessary services. Doing this reduces the attack surface.
HTTP	Hypertext Transfer Protocol. Part of the backbone of the Internet, it is a protocol used to transfer information such as the HTML and JavaScript code of web sites and applications.
ICMP	Internet Control Message Protocol. A service that makes systems discoverable by using the ping command.
Integrity	A security tenant focused on the assurance that data or documents have not experienced unauthorized changes, tampering, or destruction.
KISS	Keep it Simple, Sir. An approach to design and programming that is used to minimize complexity. There is a direct correlation between complexity and the number of bugs and vulnerabilities found in software.
Least Privilege	Limiting the permissions that a subject has on an object, based on what actions the subject is required to perform. This is also known as "need to know."
Open Design	Relying on a solid design, not the secrecy of the design,

	to provide security.
Permissions Snowball	A phenomenon seen at many organizations where employees who have been there the longest also have the most access. This is because privileges have not been updated and removed to reflect changes in the positions held by said employee.
Residual Risk	The risk that remains after applying security controls. The residual risk needs to be at an acceptable level.
SOC	Security Operations Center. This is an area in an organization dedicated to security monitoring, analysis, and event and incident response. It is staffed by security professionals and may have a command center "look and feel" that includes dashboards displayed on walls and located in a physically-restricted area.
Security Theater	Implementing security controls for the sake of being able to state that security controls have been implemented, even though their actual value is not proven or known. This runs the risk of adding unnecessary complexity.
Separation of Duties	Not granting a single individual the ability to perform a series of actions that could provide the opportunity to commit insider fraud or attacks.
Social Engineering	Manipulating someone by exploiting trust. Playing on emotions and using enticement or fear to get the victim to perform an action like click a link, open an email attachment, or provide sensitive information to an attacker.

SECTION ONE: PROTECT

"We foresee an ongoing series of low-to-moderate level cyber-attacks from a variety of sources over time, which will impose cumulative costs on US economic competitiveness and national security."

James Clapper, Director of National Intelligence [4]

This section discusses the various solutions, controls and processes that can be used by an information security team to help protect an organization from cyber attacks. This list is not comprehensive, nor is it meant to be. The goal is to provide a list of options whose implementation supports the foundation of an effective security program. Though there are continually new solutions being developed to combat ever-evolving threats, this section focuses on core solutions that address most attacks that a typical organization regularly faces.

The following items also have a maturity level indicator, which is based on the resources and expertise required to implement the respective control, as well as how fundamental it is to an InfoSec program. If an organization is just starting to build an information security department, then level 1 items are the ones to start with. As the program improves and matures, level 2 and 3 become more appropriate.

1.1 ENDPOINT PROTECTION

The days of a heterogeneous environment are gone. Endpoints come in a variety of shapes and sizes, including:

- Servers
- Desktops
- Laptops
- Mobile phones

- Tablets

Just as the form factor of endpoints can vary greatly, the list of operating systems running on these devices include:

- Mac OS
- Android
- Chrome OS
- Apple iOS
- Various distributions of Linux

Add to this the explosive growth of cloud computing and the Internet of Things (IoT), and the result is controlled chaos. Yet all of this somehow must work together and facilitate productivity, while doing it securely.

Though the IT landscape continues to grow more complex and fragmented, security fundamentals still apply. Protection solutions that can be installed on an endpoint include Anti-virus (AV), Host-based Intrusion Prevention Systems (HIPS), Host-based Intrusion Detection System (HIDS), and file integrity checkers (FIC). While each offers a different approach to protection in support of a defense in depth strategy, there is the challenge of having several solutions coexist peacefully on the same device. Software conflicts can cause performance degradations, errors, and other issues that can be frustrating for end users. Some compatibility issues may even cause security controls to fail to work properly, and perhaps not at all. Therefore, attention needs to be paid to the interoperability of the endpoint protection software, the operating system, and the applications that need to run. Issues like these may even affect the choice of security solutions that end up being deployed to endpoints.

The following solutions are described separately, but there are also several vendors that offer "bundled" solutions. When evaluating these products, consider everything offered by the bundle solution versus focusing on a single feature. It may prove more cost effective to select a product that offers several security controls. However, with bundled products make sure that the quality of all the features sought are at an acceptable level. The quality of a needed control should not be sacrificed for the sake of getting several at once.

An organization may also want to include free and open source products in the evaluation process. Just because a security product is paid for doesn't mean that it is better than something available as open- source software. There may be a longer support tail for open source solutions, however, as the entity using the product may also be solely responsible for supporting, maintaining and updating it. But with what is lost in support may be made up for in flexibility, robustness (number of features) and customization options. As open source solutions often require unique employees who can support such products, an organization may defer to vendor-provided solutions so that they can rely on the vendor-provided support that comes with it. The cost difference, in the long-term, may be worth it.

Once security controls are installed on a device, there is still no guarantee that the software will be used nor running effectively. If the user rejects or can bypass the security installed on an endpoint, it's possible that the device may actually be worse off than having no security software installed on it. Because when security software is installed on a device, that device is often put "out of mind". The device is assumed to be fully protected by having security software installed on it. Meanwhile, if the user has disabled the protection software, or if it not running correctly, the device is still vulnerable. Trust but verify. Ensure that the security software is running correctly, that it cannot be disabled, and that it does not interfere with how the user does his or her work.

1.1.1 CONFIGURATION MANAGEMENT DATABASE (CMDB)

Level 1 - The first step in protecting endpoints is to identify them. One of the most dangerous things on a network is a rogue, unmanaged device whose patch level and security posture is unknown. Maintaining an inventory of devices makes it easier to identify those that are not authorized or are not secure enough to be on the network.

Take the time to properly discover and document all assets. These include servers, workstations, network equipment, and mobile devices. Start with the production network, but do not exclude other environments such as test, development and staging. The result is an asset database, also known as a configuration management database (CMDB). A CMDB is a centralized repository of asset information.

Creating a CMDB and process to follow to keep its information current should be one of the first steps taken before the deployment of any security solutions. Doing this will ensure that all assets are protected. To keep the inventory information current, other teams such as IT operations and networking should be required to update the database as changes occur. Asset owners should be held responsible for entering and maintaining information about the devices that they are responsible for. If changes are made to an asset, such as being decommissioned, an update to the

CMDB should be done. This will help ensure that everyone has access to the latest information about what is on the network. Having current and relevant information is key to providing effective security. Creating a CMDB is the easy part. Maintaining it is the challenge.

Entries in a CMDB need a certain level of detail to be useful. Here is an example of the attributes each entry should have:

- Asset name
- Asset type
- Owner
- Description
- Operating system
- IP Address

A CMDB is only as good as its content. Therefore, ideally, it should be mandated that all asset owners review the CMDB on a regular basis and ensure that the information regarding assets they are responsible for is current. Part of the process for implementing new assets, or removing them from the network, should also be to update the CDMB. The effort spent maintaining asset information will prove its value both in terms of security and effective change management. Because maintaining an asset database is fundamental to any effective information security program, it is considered a level 1 security objective.

1.1.2 ANTI-VIRUS (AV)

Level 1 - Anti-Virus (AV) is a security solution that has one the longest histories in endpoint protection. Due to its signature-based approach of identifying malicious software, its relevance has diminished over time to the point that organizations like Netflix have discontinued its use so that resources can be focused on more effective security controls. [5]

Figure 1.1: An endpoint protection agent is installed and runs on the device, with the option of sending security alerts to a centralized log repository.

The reason for the growing irrelevance of anti-virus software is that malware creators have discovered innovative ways to defeat signature-based detection by employing techniques such as polymorphism, which results in malware that is unique to each installation. The signature database used by AV can't keep up with all the new malware strains and permutations that are discovered daily.

Many still believe that AV still provides value as it handily detects and quarantines legacy viruses, worms and Trojans that have been plaguing PCs since before the Morris worm began defining the threat landscape almost 30 years ago. [6] These legacy threats still exist, even though not nearly as effective as their modern counterparts. For example, a maker of police bodycams was discovered to be shipping products with the Conficker-B virus pre-installed (malware which wreaked havoc in 2008. [7]) It was partially effective in spreading because newer cyber security controls do not protect against this "ancient" malware.

As long as samples from the malware museum continue to popup occasionally in the wild, it will still be some time until AV no longer has any protection value. Therefore, it continues to be a fundamental component of most information security programs and is considered a level 1 security objective.

1.1.3 HOST BASED INTRUSION DETECTION SYSTEM (HIDS)

Level 2 - A host-based intrusion detection system (HIDS) is a software agent that runs on the device, providing alerts if threats are detected. HIDS monitors several different properties of a device, including:

- Software processes that are running
- Objects loaded into memory
- Network activity
- Changes made to the underlying operating system such as Windows registry settings or system file changes

HIDS is watching for behaviors that are suspicious, such as actions associated with previously-detected malware, or actions that are a- typical (otherwise known as anomalous behavior.) This is because the signature matching approach commonly used in AV is no longer effective. Since new malware variants and variations pop up every day (as many as 1 million per day per a 2015 study [8]), it is difficult to specify exactly what malware looks like anymore. HIDS tries to take a more heuristic approach for making detection possible.

Because of the challenge of tuning a HIDS to reduce the chance of false positives, it is considered a level 2 security objective.

1.1.4 HOST BASED INTRUSION PREVENTION SYSTEM (HIPS)

Level 2 - An easy way to think about host intrusion prevention system (HIPS) is as HIDS with teeth. Instead of just detecting malicious activity on a device, HIPS also has the ability to prevent that activity from taking place. HIPS offers not just a detective control, but a protection control as well.

With the additional ability to block actions, HIPS could easily mistakenly identify benign activities as malicious and act. These are known as false positives. Therefore, it takes a certain level of confidence in the protection software to allow it to autonomously take these sort of actions

There are many examples of legitimate changes taking place, such as the installation of patches, that were mis-identified and resulted in catastrophic events such as the Windows BSOD (blue screen of death), which quickly spread across enterprises like a cobalt fire.[9] This errant patch had to be quickly rolled back and caused Microsoft some embarrassment for having failed to test the patch more thoroughly. This also provided a valuable lesson. Best intentions aside, any change runs the risk of breaking something.

When implementing HIPS, it is recommended to run it first in detect- only mode for a training period of around 30-90 days. During this period the software will generate alerts when it detects something that it would have otherwise acted on if it were in protect mode. This way, a human can make the final decision whether or not the action should have actually been taken and tune the product accordingly. This learning period provides the opportunity to filter out the false positives and tune the software to the point that it is safe enough to enable its protection capabilities.

Because of the challenge of tuning a HIPS to reduce the chance of false positives, it is considered a level 2 security objective.

1.1.5 FILE INTEGRITY CHECKER (FIC)

Level 3 - A file integrity checker (FIC) monitors specific files on a device for unauthorized changes. Critical system files, whose alteration could result in system compromise, is a good place to start. However, files change all the time on a device. The key is to determine which files are worth monitoring from a security standpoint and making the FIC aware when authorized changes are going to take place to prevent false positives from being triggered.

Ideally, your organization has a base image of all operating systems used on the production network. This helps identify what the system files should look like. Any difference between the base image version of a file, and what resides on a device, should be investigated to rule out malicious activity. The FIC can do these comparisons.

An FIC runs on a device and takes regular (e.g. daily) fingerprints of the files being monitored. This fingerprint is often in the form of a checksum, otherwise known as a hash value. Any change in a file will result in a completely different hash value compared to the fingerprint of the file before the change.

```
04/11/2018   06:34  PM     245,760  adsldp.dll
04/11/2018   06:34  PM     251,904  adsldpc.dll
04/11/2018   06:34  PM      98,304  adsmsext.dll
04/11/2018   06:34  PM     341,504  adsnt.dll
04/11/2018   06:34  PM     832,512  adtschema.dll
04/11/2018   06:34  PM     142,848  AdvancedEmojiDS.dll
04/11/2018   06:34  PM     645,208  advapi32.dll
04/11/2018   06:34  PM       2,560  advapi32res.dll
04/11/2018   06:34  PM     142,336  advpack.dll
04/11/2018   06:34  PM      30,720  aeevts.dll
07/06/2018   09:20  AM     689,560  aeinv.dll
07/06/2018   02:31  AM     462,752  aepic.dll
```

Figure 1.1: There are many Windows 10 system files whose integrity you may want to monitor.

A checksum is the output of an algorithm called a one-way hashing function. Commonly used hashing algorithms are MD5 and SHA (the former is not as strong, and therefore should not be used, compared to the latter.) Using older or deprecated hashing functions runs the risk of not getting a truly unique hash value for each file. This makes file integrity checkers that use these suspect functions less effective.

Data   Hashing Algorithm   4e488d08410510a251e5352015805ed5   Hash Value (Fingerprint of Data)

Figure 1.2: Example output of OPENSSL SHA-1 hashing function, to get the hash (or fingerprint) of the Java compiler on a Mac OS device. A file serves as input to the hashing function, and the output is the hash value or fingerprint.

Figure 1.2 shows what a FIC does on a much wider scale. The FIC will also generate alerts to appropriate personnel if file changes are detected.

Files change periodically. Systems and software get updates, and patches are installed to address security vulnerabilities. Remember: if software cannot be updated, it should not be used. The reason is that no software is 100% bug-free nor 100% secure. Eventually a problem will be found that needs to get fixed, and security vulnerabilities should be patched as quickly as possible.

When software is updated, and associated files are changed as part of a planned update, the FIC should be made aware of the change in advance so it does not trigger any unnecessary alerts. Tight coordination is therefore required between the teams making changes and the team that maintains the FIC agents running on the endpoints. This way false positives will be reduced. Having this intra-team coordination can be a challenge that causes many organizations not to deploy a file integrity checking solution, despite the security benefits it can provide. Therefore, it is designated as a level 2 security objective.

1.1.6 HOST-BASED FIREWALL

A host-based firewall is a software agent that runs on a device, with the goal of preventing certain (ostensibly malicious) data from being sent to or received by the device. This section will discuss two types of host firewalls: network and web browser.

1.1.6.1 HOST-BASED NETWORK FIREWALL

Level 1 - A host-based network firewall runs on a device, with the purpose of preventing certain network-based activity from being received by the host it is running on. This type of firewall is not to be confused with a general network-based firewall, whose focus is on the entire network. The focus of a host-based network firewall is the individual device it is installed on, and these types of firewalls are bundled with most modern operating systems.

Firewalls can be set to allow traffic only from specific IP addresses and ports. A port can be referred to as a service running on a device. A web server, for example, is a service, and by default it uses port 80. By having a firewall on a device, most of the traffic inbound to the device (which includes malicious traffic) is blocked. If tuned correctly, the firewall will only allow legitimate traffic through.

When a new device gets connected to the Internet, it takes just a matter of seconds until network logs start to show evidence of scans, probes and generic attacks from IP addresses located throughout the world. To protect the device from this type of malicious activity, a firewall will block all unnecessary ports, thereby reducing the attack surface of the device.

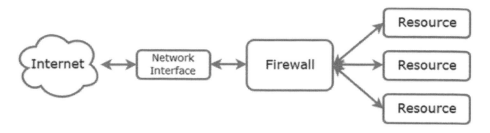

Figure 1.3: A host firewall intercepts all network traffic to and from resources on the device being protected.

The challenge of using a host-based network firewall is that it may block addresses and ports used by legitimate software on the device. Therefore, there may be some tuning required so that the balance between security and usability is assured.

Blocking unnecessary ports is fundamental to IT security, and so it is considered a level 1 security objective.

1.1.6.2 WEB BROWSER FIREWALL

Level 2 - There are several web browser add-ons (also known as extensions and plug-ins) available that prevent a device from downloading malicious content embedded within a web site. These types of add-ons can be categorized as web browser firewalls. By using this type of control, malicious content such as malvertising can be

blocked. Malvertising is the delivery of rogue web ads that have a malicious payload. Per a December 2015 article, Motherboard reported that "rogue ads had been diverting visitors from Daily Motion, one of the top 100 sites...to a malware-laden web page." [10]

A web firewall can prevent this type of malicious payload from being executed by a user's web browser or plug-ins it uses such as Adobe Flash (recently renamed Adobe Animate CC.)

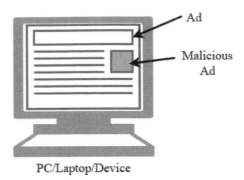

PC/Laptop/Device

Figure 1.4: Adversaries will sometimes submit malicious ads to ad providers, which are then served to and executed by a victim's web browser if no protection is in place.

The origin of many banner ads is not easily determined, and this gives cover for attackers to supply malicious content to otherwise legitimate ad providers. What is especially dangerous about malicious ads is that in many cases it does not require user action for the payload to be executed or detonated; the ad only needs to be displayed in the browser. For this reason, an organization may want an ad blocker plug-in as part of the standard software image that is deployed to endpoints. If this is not possible, consider disabling Flash by default. Ads can also be blocked by a network proxy, which is discussed later in this section.

As it can be a challenge to manage the plugins installed in web browsers on endpoint devices, this is considered a level 2 security objective.

1.1.7 OTHER HOST-BASED SECURITY SOLUTIONS

There are several security solutions that have been integrated into most operating systems, which provide a new and innovative ways to protect a device from attacks. New protection mechanisms are discovered because of analyzing past security incidents. Microsoft has received a priceless education in dealing with security issues with their software. As a result, they can be considered one of the most security aware and capability software vendors today.

The following are some of the controls that have been incorporated into many operating systems to mitigate memory-based attacks that have been seen the past.

1.1.7.1 ADDRESS SPACE LAYOUT RANDOMIZATION (ASLR)

Level 1 - Address Space Layout Randomization (ASLR) was developed in response to the way attackers could take advantage of how operating systems used memory. The adversary was able to determine where in memory objects were stored. The locations were the same regardless of what computer was used; the software loaded objects in memory the same way every time. This was due to a phenomenon of how software and operating systems used memory. This made the memory predictable, which in turn provided attackers the opportunity to manipulate objects and perform attacks.

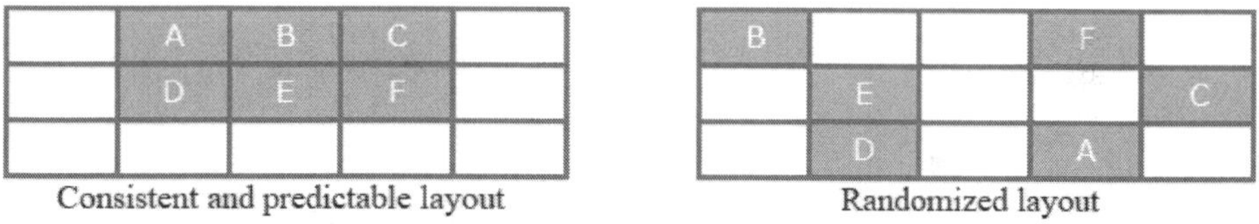

Consistent and predictable layout   Randomized layout

Figure 1.5: Before ASLR, software would store objects in memory in the exact same way, making it predictable and vulnerable to attack. ASLR randomizes objects in memory, making life more difficult for the attacker.

Because of ASLR, memory locations are randomized every time the software runs, protecting endpoints from several memory-based attacks. Since it is resident in most modern operating systems, its implementation is trivial, making it a level 1 security objective.

1.1.7.2 DATA EXECUTION PREVENTION (DEP)

Level 1 - Data Execution Prevention (DEP) is another memory-protection mechanism which is focused on the physical locations in memory where software can run. Memory, at a high level, is of two types: the stack and the heap. The stack is where programs commonly execute; the heap is where objects used by the program are stored.

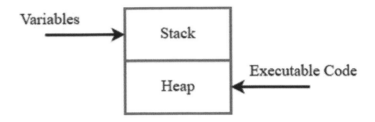

Figure 1.6: Memory at a high level is divided into the stack and the heap. Restricting where code can execute prevents certain types of memory-based attacks.

Before DEP, operating systems allowed software to run from any memory locations, which provided adversaries an opportunity. An attacker could add instructions to the storage part of memory (the heap), then exploit a vulnerability that would cause this code to execute. Because the heap was designed to be very accepting of any types of objects or data, malicious code could also be loaded (or injected) into this part of memory. Once the code was loaded, it could then be called and executed.

DEP is now integrated into many operating systems and computing devices. It runs transparently in the background, and by default, with no user interaction required. It may cause problems with the odd piece of legitimate software, but the security benefits it provides far outweigh potential compatibility issues. In most cases, it still can be disabled to accommodate the fringe program that still requires the flexibility of loading executable code into the heap. Because it is integrated transparently into most modern operating systems, it is considered a level 1 security objective.

1.1.7.3 CONTAINERIZATION, VIRTUALIZATION AND SANDBOXING

Level 3 - Another method for protecting a device from attacks is to run software in a container. This container is referred to as a sandbox or Virtual Machine (VM).

The container is virtual, meaning it is software-based, so the protection it offers is only as good as the virtualization software.

A container allows the device to run software in a space that is isolated from the host device. Each container can have its own memory and

storage that is independent of what is used and accessible by the underlying host. As a result, the operating system is not impacted if the software running inside the container (such as a web browser) becomes infected by malware.

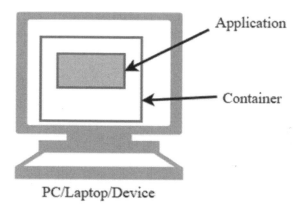

Figure 1.7: An application (guest) that runs in a container insulates the underlying operating system (host) from infection.

This approach to running programs cannot guarantee that the host is 100% insulated from what runs within the container. While that is the intent, weaknesses are occasionally found in virtualization software that makes these containers porous, exposing the underlying system to attack.

Virtualization servers host several guest VMs at the same time. These VMs could serve as the desktops used by employees instead of legacy thick-client desktops. A risk of using virtualization servers to host multiple VMs is that if one VM gets compromised, it is possible (if the virtualization software has a certain vulnerability) for the malware to have access to all the guest VMs running on the virtualization server or host.

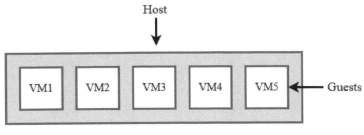

Figure 1.8: By having multiple guests hosted by a virtualization server, isolation between the VMs is possible.

Many newer operating systems automatically also use containerization (or sandboxing) natively. Newer versions of Windows, such as Windows 10, use virtual sandboxing to run programs safely, protecting the host operating system from malicious code execution. Adobe Reader (starting with version 10) launches a container for viewing PDF files (since these types of documents have for years been a popular way to deliver malicious code.) The most popular web browsers also use sandboxing to limit or defuse payloads downloaded from malicious or compromised web sites.

The risk of relying on the virtualization or sandboxing software to enforce containerization should first be understood and formally accepted. Security researcher Tom Henderson sums it up well: "Sandboxes are made of sand, not concrete." Because of the complexity involved in securely deploying a virtualization solution, it is a level 3 security objective.

1.1.8 DIGITAL CERTIFICATES

Digital certificates are a way to provide a digital identity of an entity. It is the digital equivalent of using hand-signed paper checks. To create a digital signature, a public-private key pair first needs to be created. There are several open source and vendor tools available to do this. The private key used for creating the digital certificate needs to be protected, and the certificates created should be set such that this key is non-exportable. That means the private key cannot be extracted from the certificate. If the private key can be copied, then it is difficult to verify the authenticity of anything done with the key, such as authentication or code signing.

The next step for obtaining a digital certificate is to generate a certificate request (also known as a Certificate Signing Request (CSR)). The private key is used to generate a CSR, and once created it is sent to a Certificate Authority (CA). The CA needs to be trustworthy and legitimate if you want other people, software, web browsers and operating systems to consider any certificate it creates as valid. By default, web browsers trust a slew of certificate authorities, meaning any HTTPS web site that uses a certificate signed by one of these trusted CA's is also is considered trustworthy by proxy. Tip: Have a look at the list of CA's that your web browser trusts by going to the browser settings; you might be surprised at some of the CA's that are trusted by default.

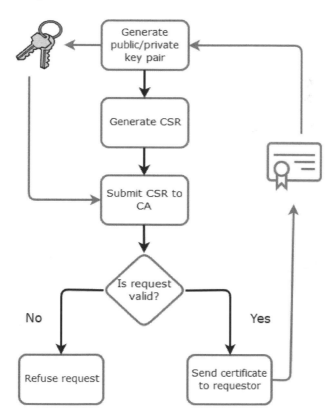

Figure 1.9: A digital certificate is created by a certificate authority in response to receiving a valid certificate signing request.

If the CSR is valid, the CA generates the digital certificate and sends it to the requestor. This certificate is now ready to use to secure web sites, sign code and emails, etc. The following are a few more topics to be familiar with when it comes to understanding digital certificates.

To learn more about how this works, it is recommended that you create your own public/private key pair and use them to create a digital certificate that you can use to sign and encrypt email. As a bonus, get your certificate signed by a trusted certificate authority (CA).

1.1.8.1 AUTHENTICATION

A signed digital certificate can be installed on a device to allow it to authenticate and connect to a network. The protocol 802.1x is the most popular way to use this form of authentication. By using this type of authentication, an organization can limit access to the network to only those devices that have the organization's digital certificate installed on it. This is also known as a "something you have" type of authentication.

For example, the organization's CA can install the network certificate on authorized devices. Any device that does not have one of these certificates will not be allowed to connect. This can prevent unauthorized or "rogue" devices from gaining access to production resources.

1.1.8.2 CODE SIGNING

Organizations should allow only approved and legitimate software to run on devices connected to the network. One way to verify that software is legitimate is to validate the digital certificate that was used by the author of the software to sign the code. Code signing provides proof that an authorized entity created and made modifications to the software. The legitimacy of the certificate (and therefore the signature) depends on the CA that issued the certificate. Certificates that are self-signed do not provide much value, since the author is basically vouching for her/himself.

Most operating systems now automatically enforce code signing validation of software. Applications that are not signed, or signed by an untrusted CA, will not be executed. In these cases, the operating system will request the user to explicitly allow the untrusted and unverified software to run, since this can pose a significant security risk.

1.1.8.3 CERTIFICATE REVOCATION LIST (CRL)

Software and operating systems can validate a digital certificate by checking its properties such as its expiration date. This validation process also needs to include a check to see if the certificate has been explicitly revoked. One reason a certificate will be revoked is if a certificate or the key used to create it has been compromised. The check for revocation is done by automatically consulting Certificate Revocation Lists (CRL.) Therefore, to support this check, network connectivity to CRL's, which are often hosted on remote servers, needs to be ensured.

Like a CRL, Microsoft operating systems use a Certificate Trust List (CTL). In September 2015, Microsoft discovered that digital certificates from a trusted vendor were leaked and used by miscreants to spoof legitimate software. [11] By having those certificates revoked, users were protected from any malware signed with those compromised certificates.

1.2 NETWORK PROTECTION

A network can be considered the circulatory system of an organization, as it provides just some of the following:

- Email
- Connectivity to printers and scanners
- Access to data repositories and cloud-based apps
- Instant messenger and chat
- Streaming music (to help us focus on work)
- Voice over IP (VoIP)
- Web browsing

Just as a network provides a conduit for legitimate activity, it is the same system that can be leveraged by adversaries to monitor activity, exfiltrate sensitive data, and install backdoors and other malware. So, it goes without saying that the security of the network is paramount.

Wi-Fi may be offered by the organization to provide Internet connectivity for employee-owned mobile devices. A recommended way to provide this Wi-Fi service is to have two separate networks: one for production access, and one for guests and personal use. While there should be monitoring in place for the production network, you may want to forego any monitoring of the guest network. The reason for this is that there may be activity that the organization does not want to be liable for. If this network is not monitored, then this provides plausible deniability if malicious, inappropriate or illegal activity is discovered to have been performed by someone utilizing this network.

Organizations are increasingly depending on cloud service providers for file and data storage, software as a service (SaaS), computational power, etc. Yet, this means using and relying on networks that are out of the organization's direct control. Trust must be extended to these providers. The challenge is being able to take advantage of everything the "cloud" provides while not increasing the risk to the organization, nor expanding its attack surface. The importance of performing a thorough review of agreements with cloud service providers cannot be overstated. Protections should be in place that prepare for worst-case scenarios, so that if catastrophe does strike (such as a data breach by a cloud service provider) the organization will be better protected and prepared to deal with it.

The following discusses several network-based security controls that are available, as well as different aspects of network-based protection.

1.2.1 FIREWALLS

A firewall is the classic example of a security device that organizations rely on for protection from network-based attacks. A firewall is commonly installed at the perimeter that separates an internal network from the Internet. Firewalls can also be installed on the internal network to provide additional protection to network segments that host sensitive resources like employee or credit card data.

The Internet perimeter is the front line, and the firewall installed at this location will routinely observe and block scans and other attacks from getting through. Firewalls, however, have evolved to do more than control the flow of individual packets. Now the term "firewall" has been extended to appliances that specifically protect databases and web applications, as well as solutions that provide several different forms of network-based protection. The following section discusses some varieties of firewalls that should be considered.

1.2.1.1 NETWORK FIREWALL

Level 1 – A network firewall is used to limit access to devices, other networks, and segments of a network. It inspects the attributes of individual packets and can analyze them in different ways. It can also operate at different network layers.

Billions of packets may traverse an organization's network every day, and each packet has several properties and layers. The Open Systems Interconnection (OSI) model was created to provide a logical view of the different layers that make up a network packet.

Layer	Description
7	Application
6	Presentation
5	Session
4	Transport
3	Network
2	Data Link
1	Physical

Table 1.1: There are seven layers to the OSI Network Model. Inspection of several layers of network packets is an example of a defense in depth strategy.

Another challenge is to not block legitimate traffic. As the primary function of a firewall is to get in the way, there will sometimes be legitimate traffic that is blocked. When one of these unintentional blocks does occur, there should be a process in place so that the issue can be researched and quickly resolved. And any changes that are made should be documented to help support and potentially roll back these changes to keep the network running.

Some organizations err on the side of security; some err on the side of availability. How much traffic a firewall blocks goes towards maintaining the balance of security versus usability. A network that is very secure but unusable is worthless to an organization, but the same could be said of the opposite.

Figure 1.10: A Network Firewall can protect against scans and attacks launched from an untrusted network.

Maintaining network firewalls is one of the most technically complicated parts of an IT infrastructure. Firewalls use policies and rules to determine which packets get blocked and which ones get to go through. These policies and rules are determined by individuals and business units within an organization and are implemented by the network operations team. The rules can quickly get very complex. Consider using a tool that provides a way to clearly manage these policies and rules, as well as graphically display the devices, networks, and the connections between them. Using a tool like this can provide documentation that is both accessible and understandable, though it goes without saying that this information should be considered sensitive (so protect it accordingly.) A network firewall is considered a fundamental part of IT security and is considered a level 1 security objective.

1.2.1.2 WEB APPLICATION FIREWALL

Level 3 – A web application firewall (WAF) can be used at the perimeter to protect web applications that face the Internet. A WAF is a security appliance that is focused on the uppermost layer of the network stack: layer 7, otherwise known as the application layer. This type of firewall examines all the requests that are sent to a web application, as well as the responses that the application returns. The WAF can block malicious content from coming or going, as well as sanitize the data so that it causes no harm on receipt.

A challenge to implementing a WAF is that this device first needs to "learn" the code of the web application it is protecting. Many WAFs have a learning mode that it can be put into for a few weeks or months at the beginning of an implementation. While in learning mode, the WAF observes web usage activity, and over time determines what "normal" looks like. This helps reduce the number of false positives the WAF reports. "Normal" is subjective because applications can be coded in myriad ways yet produce the same results. Without learning, some of these coding choices would be considered malicious to the WAF.

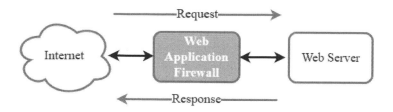

Figure 1.11: A WAF offers web-specific protection for web applications.

Another benefit of a WAF is that it can also provide virtual patching. Some applications and servers cannot be immediately patched, even in the face of zero-day vulnerabilities. A WAF can prevent attackers from being able to exploit vulnerabilities before they are properly patched by blocking these attacks from ever reaching the web application.

For example, early in 2015 a critical vulnerability in the Apache Struts2 framework was discovered. This is a framework behind many Internet web sites and applications. The cause was determined to be a flaw in the underlying language: Java. A fix for Java was not planned to be released quickly. The Apache Foundation was able to respond more rapidly however, and they did so in the form of a rule that could be applied to web servers. This prevented attacks from ever reaching the Struts2 vulnerability, thereby protecting web applications that used this framework until the Java patch was made available and installed. [12] In this example the Apache web server rule is a virtual patch, which is a tactical (short-term) fix; patching Java is the strategic (long-term) fix.

Because the implementation of a WAF requires administration by someone well versed in web application development, it is considered a level 3 security objective.

1.2.1.3 DATABASE FIREWALL

Level 3 – A database firewall is another type of layer 7 firewall that is tuned specifically to look at database-related syntax being sent to a database. This appliance usually sits in front of a database, so any commands sent to the database are first evaluated, at which point an alert may be generated and the query may be blocked. A database firewall can prevent attacks like SQL injection from reaching its intended target. However, before implementation a learning period is required so that the database firewall can learn what legitimate queries can be expected and should not be blocked.

A database firewall can protect a database that serves as a backend for an application. For example, an app may have a security vulnerability such as SQL injection, due to a lack of input validation. For vulnerable applications like this, a database firewall can be used to provide "virtual patching." This would protect the database from receiving malicious SQL statements that are not blocked by the application in front of the database.

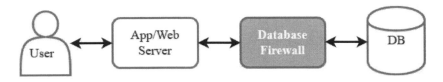

Figure 1.12: A database firewall inspects and filters commands before they reach a database.

A challenge is that structured query language (SQL) databases are being usurped by NoSQL and other non-relational databases, where the syntax is very different. Any worthy database firewall product, however, should be able to protect the latest incarnations of data repositories. As implementation of a database firewall requires someone who is very familiar with how database queries are structured, this is considered a level 3 security solution.

1.2.2 NETWORK INTRUSION PREVENTION SYSTEM (NIPS)

Level 2 - A Network Intrusion Prevention System (NIPS) is a device that monitors network traffic very similar to how a firewall inspects network packets. In most cases, the NIPS is installed at the perimeter to protect an organization's internal network from Internet-based attacks. An intrusion prevention system can be considered the next evolution of a firewall, as it does the following:

- Uses more sophisticated methods of inspecting packets
- Examines different layers of the network packets

- Evaluates a collection of several packets to identify patterns or anomalous behavior

It can be a challenge to tune a NIPS properly so that it does not alert (or even worse, block) based on false positives. The first phase of implementation should be to put the NIPS into alert-only mode so that it can be tuned so that only meaningful alerts are generated.

Figure 1.13: A NIPS monitors and can block traffic coming from the Internet before it reaches the internal network.

The earlier version of a NIPS is a network intrusion detection system (NIDS), which only provides alerts and does not have the capability to block any network traffic. A NIDS has been replaced in most cases by a NIPS, which provides the option of blocking malicious traffic. As a NIPS is considered a step above a firewall, which is fundamental to a security program, and so it is considered a level 2 security objective.

1.2.4 MALWARE PREVENTION SYSTEM (MPS)

Level 3 – An MPS (also known as a Malware Analysis Appliance) can be an effective way to prevent malicious applications or scripts from landing and executing on endpoint devices and servers. An MPS is installed at the network perimeter and needs to have a way to intercept binaries file for inspection. One way is to have the MPS interface with an email gateway so that email attachments are stripped and fed to the MPS for inspection.

An MPS is focused on the application level of network activity and examines the files that employees download during the course of the day. These files could be deliberately downloaded, or accidentally (such as clicking the wrong link in an email.). Regardless of the file or its delivery method, when downloaded, the MPS makes a copy of the file and executes (or detonates) it in a container that the MPS starts up just to analyze the file. The analysis will observe and record the actions that the file performs, such as:

- Network connections
- What is loaded into memory
- Files that are accessed or changed
- Registry changes
- Processes that are spawned

Based on the analysis, and comparison with signatures of other known malicious files, the MPS forms a conclusion about whether the binary has evil intent or not.

However, it is possible that the first infection may not be blocked. This is because a typical implementation of an MPS is to install it so that it is not in-line; the MPS receives a copy of the attachment while the original attachment is still delivered to its intended recipient. This is because no conclusion has been made yet about the file. If an MPS does identify the file as malicious, it is an option for the MPS to then alert the email gateway or other security appliances so that any future download attempts of the same file are blocked.

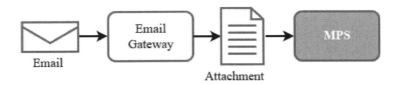

Figure 1.14: In this MPS configuration, an MPS receives a copy of binary files that are attached to emails received by the email gateway.

An MPS is a solution that should be considered only after more fundamental security controls have been implemented and have proven to be effective in contributing to the overall security of the organization. If that is the case, then an MPS makes an excellent addition to an organization's information security arsenal. Since an MPS is appropriate for a more seasoned and well-staffed security operations team, it is considered a level 3 security solution.

1.2.5 EMAIL GATEWAY

Level 2 - Email is one of the most effective ways to deliver malware. Once installed, it is possible for an adversary to obtain a foothold on the network and pivot to other endpoints, eventually finding their way to protected resources like databases, file shares and sensitive emails.

Figure 1.15: All email bound is first received by an email gateway for inspection and possible subsequent delivery.

An email gateway can be implemented in-line so that all emails must be analyzed and determined to be safe first before being delivered to employee inboxes. It may also be able to analyze attached files, like how an MPS runs binaries in a dedicated container. Some versions of a gateway can also analyze and sanitize any links contained in the email body.

Given that email is the most popular way for adversaries to get malware installed on a network, an email gateway may be considered a fundamental part of an organization's information security program. However, given its complexity and reliance on a seasoned email administrator to implement and operate it properly, it is considered a level 2 security objective.

1.2.6 INTERNET PROXY

Level 2 - A network proxy is an appliance that can be installed in-line between the Internet and the internal network. All Internet-bound requests, such as visits to web pages, flow through the proxy where the request is evaluated and categorized. Some examples of these categories include:

- Controlled Substances

- Gambling
- Commerce
- Phishing
- Software Downloads

The organization sets the Internet policy, which can be to block certain categories of web sites. It is an imperfect science however, and legitimate sites will occasionally be blocked. When this happens, users should have a process to request that the site be unblocked. This process should also include a security review to determine whether the site is safe to be accessed.

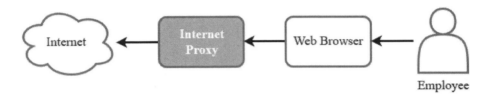

Figure 1.16: A proxy determines whether to let user web site requests proceed to the Internet.

Having a proxy in place to intercept web site requests also lets the security team explicitly add blocks to a policy in response to information (or "intel") received about sites that host a malicious payload. A web proxy should be considered essential for any organization that allows Internet access from a production network.

As there is the risk of blocking legitimate sites, and the need to have staff available for adding and removing sites in a timely manner, this is considered a level 2 security objective.

1.2.7 JUMP SERVER

Level 3 – The use of jump servers allows an organization to limit access to production systems. A jump server can also serve as the only way to provide limited access from an internal network segment to a more exposed network segment or zone, such as a DMZ. Proper implementation requires locking down the network and production systems so that the jump servers are the only interface available to access them. A jump server can provide several features, such as:

- Not granting users administrative access to production systems
- Logging commands that are executed by a user
- Limiting what commands a user can execute

A user first logs onto a jump server. Once logged on, the user can then gain access (or "jump") to one of the production systems the jump server has access to. Since all commands issued by the user are first sent to the jump server, this server can filter commands so that only certain ones are passed to the production system.

Every command that the user executes can also be logged for analysis and generating alerts. An example of an action that may generate an alert is when a user attempts to add a new account to a production system, which could indicate a breach of policy or something malicious being attempted.

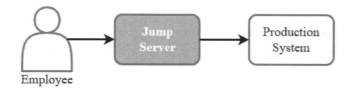

Figure 1.17: A jump server protects production systems from direct access and can log commands issued by users.

Mandating that employees access production systems only via jump servers helps limit what employees can do, and logs what actions they do (or attempt to) perform.

1.3 USER AWARENESS AND EDUCATION

Level 1 – Users are on the front line of protecting an organization. It is often not by technical means that an attacker illicitly gains sensitive info, access to systems, and footholds on a protected network. Instead, age-old methods of social engineering are often used, where the user is tricked into performing an action. People are manipulated using various techniques, often by exploiting trust and fear, so that the user does not think before acting. The goal is to get users to think first, especially when it comes to clicking links, opening attachments, or disclosing information.

Education about social engineering attacks and techniques can take several forms, including:

- Giving presentations to different groups
- Communications sent by leadership
- Sharing news stories of victims that fell prey to attacks
- Inviting law enforcement representatives to provide awareness training to groups

Phishing is the most effective way to get malware installed on devices. The installation of malware can lead to compromise of not just a single user, but potentially of the entire organization as it propagates throughout the network. Therefore, phishing awareness training should be included in an overall security awareness program.

An effective method for teaching users how to identify phish and what to do (or not do) when a phish is encountered is to leverage a phishing awareness program. This can include sending a fake email to employees and taking note of who clicked a link contained therein. There are several tools available that allow you to create these types of educational phishing campaign. These tools allow you to observe and report on the results, and even provide user awareness training to those who took the bait. SANS is one such organization which offers a phishing awareness tool as part of their Securing the Human (STH) suite of security awareness tools. [13]

Making users aware of the important role they play in protecting an organization and equipping them with the cognitive tools needed to identify and react appropriately when receiving a social engineering attack, will significantly contribute to an organization's overall security. As this is fundamental to any information security program of any size, it is considered a level 1 security objective.

1.4 SUMMARY

There are many security solutions available for protecting endpoint devices, the network and end users. Using the right combination of controls that support the security concepts discussed in the previous section helps reduce the risk of attack, and will increase the awareness of suspicious and malicious activity that may be taking place within an organization's IT systems.

The maturity level assigned to each item represents the level of maturity an organization's security team (or SOC) should be at to effectively implement the respective security control. It is recommended to pursue these security controls according to what is appropriate for your organization, and in the order of their maturity levels. The order of the items for each level does not represent their importance or the order in which they should be pursued.

1.4.1 LEVEL 1

The following are fundamental security controls, making them level 1 security objectives:

- Configuration Management Database (CMDB)
- Anti-Virus (AV)
- Host-Based Network Firewall
- Address Space Layout Randomization (ASLR)
- Data Execution Prevention (DEP)
- Network Firewall
- Security Awareness Training

1.4.2 LEVEL 2

The following should be implemented only after a solid security foundation has been established, making them level 2 security objectives:

- Host Intrusion Detection System (HIDS)
- Host Intrusion Prevention System (HIPS)
- Web Browser Firewall
- Network Intrusion Prevention System (NIPS)
- Email Gateway
- Internet Proxy

1.4.3 LEVEL 3

The following require experienced security staff and adequate resources to implement and operate, making them level 3 security objectives:

- File Integrity Checker (FIC)
- Containerization, Virtualization and Sandboxing
- Web Application Firewall (WAF)
- Database Firewall
- Malware Prevention System (MPS)
- Jump Server

1.5 TERMS AND DEFINITIONS

The following are the terms that were discussed in this section.

Term	Definition
Anomalous Behavior	Strange or unexpected behavior that could indicate malicious activity
ASLR	Address Space Layout Randomization. This is a control implemented by PC hardware and operating systems to randomize how data objects are stored in memory. This mitigates certain types of memory-manipulation attacks.
Attack Surface	A description or how susceptible or exposed a target is to attack.
AV	Anti-Virus. A software agent that runs on a device, with the intent to protect it from malicious software. It is often signature-based, making it perhaps less effective than newer types of security controls.
BYOD	Bring Your Own Device. Organizations offer their employees an opportunity to use a personal device to connect to a production network. This is usually done by using containerization software on the device that provides a virtual separation of work and personal

	data.
CA	Certificate Authority. A trusted entity that issues certificates in response to certificate requests.
Checksum	See Hash Value.
Cloud Computing	A room full of servers somewhere on the Earth, and not floating above it.
CMDB	Configuration Management Database. A centralized repository of information about IT assets, such as computers and servers, that needs to kept current in order to be effective.
Containerization	Running applications with resources (memory, CPU, etc.) that are isolated from the underlying host operating system.
CRL	Certificate Revocation List. This is a list of digital certificates that have been revoked for various reasons, such as being no longer trusted or expired. This list is maintained and globally available.
CSR	Certificate Signing Request. A request issued to a certificate authority (CA) for a digital certificate. A certificate issued from a trusted CA should be considered more secure than a self-signed certificate.
Decommission	To securely retire a device so that it is no longer on the network and no longer in use.
DEP	Data Execution Prevention. This is a control implemented by computer hardware and operating systems to mitigate certain types of memory-manipulation attacks.
Deprecated	Something that is out of date, whose use is no longer recommended. A newer version, or its replacement, should be used instead.
Detective Control	A sensor focused on identifying certain behavior(s) taking place, at which point it can notify the user and/or security personnel.
Digital Certificate	A digital "something you have" form of authentication.
DMZ	Demilitarized zone. A segment of a network that sits between an internal (trusted) network and the network segment that hosts Internet-facing servers. This helps protect internal resource from Internet-based attacks.
Exfiltrate	To leak sensitive data out to the Internet or to

	unauthorized individuals.
False Positive	Something that is errantly considered to be negative, but after further investigation it is concluded to be benign.
FIC	File Integrity Checker. A software agent that runs on a device to help ensure the integrity of critical files.
Hash Value	The unique fingerprint of a file after running it through a one-way hashing algorithm such as SHA-256.
HIDS	Host Based Intrusion Detection System. Monitoring software that watches and issues alerts when malicious network traffic reaches the device.
HIPS	Host Based Intrusion Prevention System. Same as HIDS, but with the added benefit of being able to block traffic from reaching the device.
Internet of Things (IoT)	Devices of all shapes and sizes that are connected to the Internet.
Jump Server	Preventing direct access to servers by mandating that users log onto an intermediary server which provides limited and logged access to the target server.
Malvertising	Malicious web-based advertising such as banner ads that contain a malicious payload that infects the web browser displaying the ad.
MD5	Message Digest Algorithm 5. A cryptographic hash algorithm used to verify the integrity of files and data. It is popular but no longer considered a secure option.
Miscreants	Adversaries, attackers and malicious actors.
MPS	Malware Prevention Solution (or System). An appliance or service that receives files (such as email attachments) and analyses them by running the file in a sandbox. What the file does as far as network connections, objects loaded into memory, registry changes it makes, etc. help determine whether the file is malicious or not. This is a signature-less or behavioral analysis form of malware identification.
NIDS	Network Intrusion Detection System. A system installed at the network perimeter that analyses network traffic to identify malicious traffic, and issue alerts if malicious activity is detected.

NIPS	Network Intrusion Prevention System. A system installed at the network perimeter that analyses network traffic to identify malicious traffic, and issue alerts if malicious activity is detected. It has an advantage over NIDS in that it can also block traffic that is considered malicious.
OSI	Open Systems Interconnection. A standards body whose purpose is to help standardize protocols so that they can be explained in a way that is more easily understandable.
Polymorphism	Changing the properties of an executable file (or binary) so that it evades signature-based detection.
Protection Control	A security control that blocks actions determined to be malicious from taking place. Also known as a preventative or protective control.
Proxy	An appliance or service that serves as an intermediary between an end user device and the Internet. Its purpose is to restrict Internet access to only those sites that the proxy deems safe and appropriate, which can be based on the organization's policy.
SHA-1	Secure Hash Algorithm 1, a cryptographic hashing algorithm that can be used to verify the integrity of files and data. It is recommended over MD5.
SHA-2	Secure Hash Algorithm 2, a newer cryptographic hashing algorithm designed by the NSA that is recommended over MD5 and SHA-1.
SQL	Structured Query Language. The syntax used by most major relational database vendors to interact with the data and structure of a database.
Trojan	Software that disguises itself as benign or beneficial, but in actuality contains a malicious payload.
Virtual Patching	Protection provided by an appliance such as a WAF that prevents attackers from exploiting vulnerabilities in an application or system before a patch is available or applied.
Virus	Malicious software with the intent to spread and infect hosts.
VM	Virtual Machine. A software-based container that runs on top of a host operating system. The container can

	run its own instance of software or an operating system in a way that insulates the underlying host from any infections the VM may experience.
WAF	Web Application Firewall. A security appliance that is installed in front of a web application to block malicious requests. A WAF can also provide "virtual patching" to mitigate vulnerabilities that cannot be immediately patched.
Worm	Software created with the primary intent to spread to as many hosts as possible.
XSS	Cross–Site Scripting. A type of attack that a web application may be vulnerable to due to insecure JavaScript code.
Zero Day Vulnerability	A weakness in software that is known to adversaries but not to the software manufacturer. Also known as an "O day."

SECTION TWO: DETECT

"The world is full of obvious things which nobody by any chance ever observes."

Sherlock Holmes

One of the greatest fears of any security professional is that there is malicious activity going on undetected somewhere on the network. Stealth is one of the main modus operandi of attackers and how the majority of malware behaves. An Advanced Persistent Threat (APT) is malware that persists on a network to observe and report, for an extended period and without notice. An interesting definition of APT comes from the security vendor Damballa: "Advanced Persistent Threats (APTs) are a cybercrime category directed at business and political targets. APTs require a high degree of 'stealthiness' over a prolonged duration of operation to be successful. The attack objectives therefore typically extend beyond immediate financial gain, and compromised systems continue to be of service even after key systems have been breached and initial goals reached." [14]

This section discusses the detective form of security, where sensors generate alerts for security personnel to respond to. The response taken should have the following attributes:

- Pre-defined
- Documented
- Rehearsed
- Communicated to the team
- Periodically reviewed
- Kept current

Security alerts that do not have a defined response have debatable value and may just end up providing noise and distracting busy work.

To be able to rely on security controls to provide constant real-time monitoring, assurance that those sensors are running is needed. The monitors need monitors, in other words. Just because an alert (such as from a scan or perceived attack) is not sounded, a security event could still be taking place. To paraphrase the famous saying: "If a tree falls in a forest but there is no one there to hear it, the tree still fell, there just wasn't a working sensor to observe it."

An uptime monitor, such as a heartbeat, can play an important part of the implementation of any security control. This heartbeat monitors the health and continuous operation of a sensor. A dashboard can be set up

to display the status of heartbeats, and an overview of the health of all of the sensors deployed to the network and endpoints can be provided.

The focus of this section is the tactics, techniques and procedures (TTP) that can be used to assist with the detection of security events. Defensive tactics can include the implementation of individual controls, or of a larger security solution that provides various sensors. The techniques and procedures used by a security team should be clearly defined, documented and rehearsed before sensors are enabled and generating alerts. The worst time to determine how to respond to a security alert is when the response is needed.

As with section one, each of the following security controls have a security maturity level indicator, which is based on the item's implementation and maintenance complexity and cost, as well as how fundamental the item is to the foundation of a typical organization's information security program.

2.1 CONTINUOUS MONITORING

Continuous monitoring provides a constant awareness of what is taking place on the network and all endpoints connected to it. This awareness is provided by sensors that are installed on endpoints and at various places throughout the network. These sensors generate security alerts and monitoring information that can be collected by a centralized log repository like a Security Information and Event Management (SIEM.) Based on rules, the SIEM will generate alerts based on certain events that it receives. A SIEM provides aggregation, alert generation, and a "single pane of glass" view of alerts received from multiple, disparate devices, all in real-time.

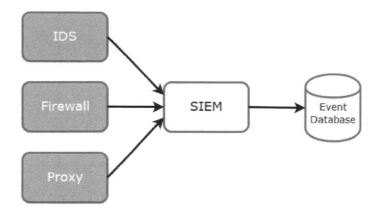

Figure 2.1: An event repository like a SIEM can receive alerts and log information from multiple sensors in real time.

When receiving and processing security alerts, there are two rules that should be considered:

- If an alert is not generated or received, it does not necessarily indicate the absence of an event
- If an alert is generated, it should not be assumed that it will automatically be observed or responded to

Once a sensor is installed, it should be considered the equivalent of a living entity in that it requires its own monitoring and maintenance, to help ensure that it continues to perform as expected, and that it can be relied on when it is needed most. Along those lines, here are a couple of scenarios that you want to avoid:

- "We installed a sensor correctly but were not aware that it stopped running."
- "Our sensor was running correctly at the time, but no one saw the alerts."

As sensors are computing devices unto themselves, they have certain attributes that can be monitored, such as those listed in the following table:

Property	Details
Storage space	Is the hard disk running out of space?
CPU utilization	Is there some sort of infinite loop or resource exhaustion event that is causing the CPU to max out?

Memory consumption	Is there a memory leak that is causing all available memory to be used?
Network ping	Is the system reachable via the network or the Internet?

Table 2.1: There are several system properties that can be monitored to help ensure system uptime.

For system health monitoring, one way to generate a heartbeat is to send the sensor a test event. This event should flow through to the SIEM. The heartbeat generator could be a perpetually running script whose only job is to periodically create a test (or heartbeat) event (e.g. every 60 seconds.) The SIEM can be set up with rules to handle any "heartbeat" events it receives. If the SIEM does not catch the event, then it's "Houston, we have a problem."

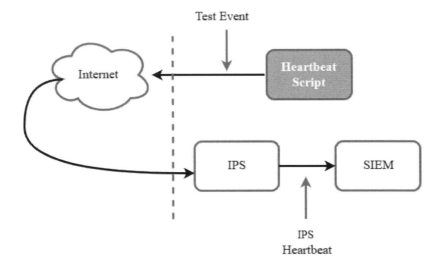

Figure 2.2: A heartbeat can be used to ensure an IPS is alive and well and can be relied on to send alerts when needed.

Using heartbeat scripts to monitor the health of sensors is not a perfect solution, as the script itself can fail due to various reasons, such as those listed in Table 2.1. Therefore, it is advisable that the heartbeat scripts themselves are monitored in some way. This could be in the form of a separate monitoring process or script that helps ensure that the heartbeats themselves are running reliably.

2.1.1 ALERTS

Level 1 – Most SIEM solutions provide the ability to perform a specific action based on receiving an alert from a security device. Examples of these actions can include sending an email or adding an item to a dashboard. The response actions taken by a SIEM need to get the attention of security analysts so that they are responded to quickly. If the SIEM will be sending notifications, the organization's existing messaging solution should be leveraged if possible. This could be the organization's email infrastructure or a simple messaging service (SMS). The information contained in these notifications should be reviewed from a confidentiality standpoint to ensure sensitive information is not inappropriately disclosed. This review should include asking questions such as:

- What if the contents of the message ended up in the wrong person's inbox?
- What could be done with that information?
- Who else could benefit from receiving this notification?

Using a system that can automatically create notifications for individuals and teams runs the risk of sending too many notifications and overwhelming its recipients. A SIEM can create a security event based on the alerts it receives. The event needs to actionable however; otherwise it may only serve as distracting noise. If an event gets the attention of an analyst, it had better be worth the time of that valuable security resource. Therefore, there needs to be a balance between the volume of events, and the finite resources available to respond to them. This is where prioritization comes in. A severity or priority rating (e.g. 1 to 5, where 5 is most severe) can be assigned to each event to help the analyst and team decide which events deserve immediate attention, and which ones can wait.

Remember: "If everything is a priority, then nothing is a priority."

If there are too many events to be handled appropriately, security personnel may start to become desensitized and start tuning them out. Event apathy appears to have contributed to the expensive and widely- publicized incident suffered by Target Corporation in 2013, where alerts generated by a malware prevention appliance were not seen (and therefore not responded to) by security personnel until it was too late. [15] Also, keep in mind that distraction is sometimes part of the adversary's TTP. This is also known as misdirection. The attacker may cause an incident, such as a distributed denial of service (DDoS) attack, in order to draw the attention of a security team away from another attack (such as information theft.) Ideally there will be security resources available to respond to both the primary and secondary events.

Once an event notification is received, what happens next should be determined in advance. The response taken should be captured in a document (known as a use case) that is accessible by all security staff who may be called on to handle similar events in the future. The use case should be communicated and made available to the security team and reviewed periodically to ensure it continues to be relevant and current. Just as the security landscape constantly fluctuates and evolves, so do the use cases employed by a security team.

Security sensors and solutions should be set up so that they generate alerts. These alerts provide awareness and actionable events for the security team to respond to. Therefore, due to the essential nature of security alerts, they are considered a level 1 security objective.

2.1.2 SECURITY INFORMATION AND EVENT MANAGEMENT (SIEM)

Level 2 - A Security Information and Event Management solution (referred to as a SIEM from this point forward) provides a couple of main benefits. First, it provides a centralized location to collect log files from disparate sources. Appliances and sensors like IPS, firewalls, Internet proxies, databases and servers can send events to a SIEM. A SIEM is flexible enough so that it can receive events from almost anything that can generate and send information to a specified IP address and port. Connectors are established to provide the conduit between a logging source and the SIEM.

A SIEM is also a powerful tool for mining and correlating thousands to trillions of data. This can be done automatically in real-time, or as a background process, and alerts and dashboards can be generated based on rules provided by the vendor or developed by members of the security team.

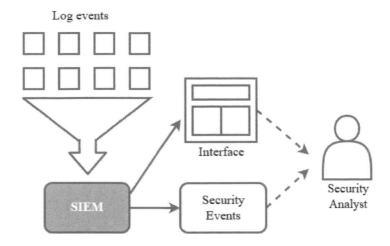

Log events

Figure 2.3: Events from various systems can be collected by a SIEM.

Using a SIEM makes the activity of finding interesting and potentially malicious activity more efficient because all the log files are in one location where events from several different systems can be correlated and aggregated. A key element to being able to tie events together is to have the clocks of all reporting systems synchronized. Network Time Protocol (NTP) can be used, which uses a central time server that all networked systems can leverage. As a result, all systems use the same clock, and all log events will have a synchronized timestamp that allows for the accurate correlation of events across multiple and disparate systems.

By having the ability to connect events from different systems, a security analyst gains a complete picture. For example: a sequence of packets was received by a firewall, passed to an IPS, then finally received by a web server, resulting in a XSS attack. Synchronized event timestamps provides an accurate end-to-end history of what happened, which can make analysis easier and response quicker.

A SIEM solution enables an organization to have a consolidated view of security events from disparate systems. Using heartbeats with the SIEM can help ensure that security controls and sensors are up and running and utilizing NTP ensures that the log events are synchronized.

While a SIEM can provide immense value to an organization, it does require a more seasoned professional to implement it so that it can be used effectively. For this reason, it is considered a level 2 security objective.

2.1.3 REPORTING

Level 1 – A challenge of most information security programs is communicating the value that the program provides to the organization.

That is because when it comes to security, no news is good news. However, no news can be seen by others as a poor use of money and resources. It is therefore critical to be able to communicate the value that the information security team provides to the organization, and to do so on a regular basis, even if significant security events or incidents have not taken place. An effective report is:

- Repeatable
- Based on facts (quantitative)
- Provides a clear message
- Is tailored to the intended audience

Reports should be created which show the alerts, events and incidents the team has addressed, and attacks that were mitigated. It matters how "attack" is defined. Scans happen all the time; is this just Internet noise or an actual precursor to something more nefarious? How security appliances define attacks, and the severity they assign various alerts, varies greatly. The message you are trying to convey with the report will help determine whether or not it is helpful to categorize scans as attacks.

Reports can serve to support an organization's information security program. Taking the time to make sure the reports are objective, clearly convey a message to the intended audience, and are reproducible in an automated way, can help ensure that an information security program will continue to get the support and resources required to be effective. Communication is essential to convey the value an IT security team provides to an organization. Therefore, it is considered a level 1 security objective.

2.2 NETWORK ACTIVITY

There are several different kinds of network activity that should be monitored. Being aware of certain events, or combinations of events, could lead to the detection of malware installations, attacks, scans, and other unwanted activities. The following discusses some of the network activity that you may want to monitor as part of protecting your own organization.

2.2.1 DNS QUERY MONITORING

Level 3 – Domain Name Resolution (DNS) is a mechanism that saves people from having to remember an IP address (a series of numbers) in order to reach a web site. While DNS is helpful today with the ubiquity of IPv4 addresses (in n.n.n.n notation), this tool will prove essential once the Internet has transitioned to IPv6, which uses eight groups of four hexadecimal digits [16] like fe80::b089:75ff:fefd:47a4. Try memorizing that!

Today, to visit www.google.com, the web browser resolves this domain name into an IPv4 address (e.g. 8.8.8.8). This address serves as the location of the server hosting Google's web site. There are thousands of DNS servers across the Internet that perform the resolution of domains into IP addresses for web sites and services all over the globe. The problem is that DNS was created in the early days of the Internet, when people were more concerned about connectivity than security.

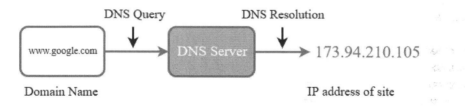

Figure 2.4: A DNS query is made to resolve an easy to remember domain name to a harder to remember IP address.

DNS hijacking is, at a high level, an attack where the DNS record for a web site is changed so that a victim is redirected to a compromised site (which may host a malicious payload.) So, if the DNS record for www.google.com was hijacked, for example, instead of going to Google, people could instead be redirected to a site pretending to be Google but in actuality is a site laden with malware or asking the user for sensitive information.

Monitoring the DNS queries that take place on the network can also be an effective way to detect infected devices. Several different strains of malware will connect to Internet servers (known as Command and Control (C&C) servers) to receive instructions, download additional modules or payloads, or upload the sensitive data it pilfers. The domain names of many of these sites is known through the sharing of cyber intelligence. Watching for any DNS queries to these malicious domains can be a good indicator of infected devices on the network.

Implementing DNS monitoring is non-trivial and should only be considered after more fundamental security solutions have already been implemented and are proving their value. For this reason, DNS monitoring is considered a level 3 security objective.

2.2.2 DATA LOSS PREVENTION

Level 2 – "Preventing the exfiltration of sensitive data, such as confidential information, customer data, or intellectual property, relies on monitoring data and documents that are sent from a trusted internal network to the Internet. A Data Loss Prevention (DLP) monitoring and prevention solution should therefore be set up to watch any points where the two networks intersect, such as perimeter Internet gateways. These solutions look for certain textual content and documents such as:

- Strings and numbers that looks like social security or credit card numbers
- Electronic documents that contain proprietary information
- Presentations that are labeled as confidential
- Any encrypted files sent by a contractor (non-FTE)

A growing challenge to DLP monitoring is the blurring of the perimeter. This is due in large part to the increasing use of cloud service providers. Another challenge is the increasing use of encryption for everyday use, for both data at rest and in transit. The contents of encrypted files and communications are unable to be inspected.

Figure 2.5: A DLP solution monitors traffic leaving a network to alert on and prevent sensitive data from leaving the network.

Cloud providers are sensitive to concerns about security and ensuring the confidentiality of protected data. Most provide controls to ensure data separation and the use of activity logging. These controls should be reviewed carefully as part of the overall evaluation of any cloud hosting provider being considered for use by an organization.

For using DLP with encryption there are also options, such as blocking encrypted files from being emailed by non-FTEs or doing a man-in- the-middle implementation of DLP where traffic is first decrypted and inspected, then re-encrypted before exiting the Internet gateways (though this method has its own privacy and security concerns.)

Protection against inbound attacks should be implemented and providing value to an organization before looking at monitoring and preventing sensitive data from being leaked. Because of this, DLP is considered a level 2 security objective.

2.2.3 ANONYMIZER NETWORK MONITORING

Level 3 - The Onion Router (TOR) network and the Invisible Internet Project (I2P) provide networks that can be used to proxy Internet traffic, which renders individuals "anonymous" as they browse the web. The word "anonymous" is in quotes because there is some debate about just how anonymous people really are when using TOR. Regardless, this network is used ostensibly to preserve privacy, but is also being increasingly used by malware to hide activity, such as data exfiltration and downloading instructions and payloads from C&C servers. Individuals may also be leveraging TOR at work, but from the organization's perspective there are some risks to allowing this. For example, usage may:

- Provide a channel that allows for the exfiltration of sensitive data
- Implicate the organization in illegal activity such as downloading protected content

Everyone has the right to be anonymous on the Internet. A large percentage of anonymizer network usage is benign (you can buy homemade cookies using TOR and Bitcoin, for example [17]). However, here we are talking about an organization preventing potentially malicious activity on its network.

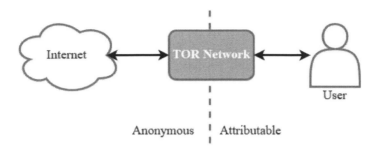

Figure 2.6: The Internet activity is ostensibly non-attributable when using an anonymizer network.

By being aware of the different anonymizer networks that may be used for malicious purposes, correct monitoring can be put in place to gain awareness if any activity involving IP addresses associated with these networks is taking place. The monitoring can be done by maintaining a list of current TOR exit nodes, and there are several open-source sites that provide this. It should be noted that the IP addresses used by these networks constantly change, so the list used for monitoring should also be refreshed on a regular (e.g. hourly) basis. Identifying endpoints on the network that are connecting to these IP addresses may point to a compromised device, or an insider threat that is covering his or her tracks.

A script could be created that downloads this list of IP addresses on an hourly basis, then adds those IP addresses to a lookup table in the SIEM. With a dashboard or alert set up, it is possible to be notified whenever someone (or something) visits an anonymizing network. Anonymizer network monitoring may be considered to be more in the research realm of IT security, as it is a recent development in malware discovery, and its value is not guaranteed. For this reason, fundamentals should first be focused on, making this a level 3 security objective.

2.2.4 HONEYPOTS

Level 3 - A honeypot is a host or server on the network that appears, for all intents and purposes, to be just another legitimate asset on the network. Or it could be dressed up to be more attractive to adversaries, by hosting files with names like salaries.xls or passwords.txt. The goal is to actually be targeted by attackers. This is because the purpose of a honeypot is to provide information about the different attacks that the organization is potentially exposed to. Observing attacks against a honeypot could also reveal an insider threat, such as an employee who copies sensitive files and uploads them to the Internet. Honeypots can also distract and occupy the attention of attackers, "thus making them think they're getting away with something, when in reality they're chasing their tails." [18]

There is some debate whether the use of a honeypot is entrapment. But it could be argued that while a honeypot provides opportunity, it is still the adversary that deliberately performs the malicious action and should therefore be held responsible for doing more than just falling for a trap.

The use of honeypots should be explored only after the fundamentals have been implemented and proven effective. For this reason, a honeypot is considered a level 3 security objective.

2.3 VULNERABILITY SCANNING

Level 2 – Vulnerability scanning serves two purposes: evaluating assets for their security hardiness and identifying all endpoints that are connected to the network.

A common process for vulnerability scanning is to first do a network scan. This is useful for asset identification, including finding those items that are not documented or previously known. These could be rogue endpoints, or devices that have been installed for legitimate purposes, but not with consent nor awareness of the security team. Assets that are discovered and determined to be legitimate should be documented in a repository such as a configuration management database (see CMDB in Section 1 of this book.) Rogue devices should be found and removed from the production network ASAP.

The next step is to iterate the list of discovered assets and perform a more detailed scan of each. This is known as an asset scan, which can be very useful for finding patching opportunities. Caution should be used however, as a scan could cause the target to fail due to it being subjected to an excessive amount of network activity that a scan can generate. Some assets may need to be exempt from scanning to avoid them from crashing, though it can be said that a scan that crashes a system identifies a system that is prone to denial of service attacks.

There are two types of asset scans: authenticated and non- authenticated. Authenticated scans require the scanner to log onto the device, which provides much more access for the scanner and therefore more detailed scan coverage (e.g. able to see software versions that are installed on the device, etc.). An account that follows the principle of least privilege should be created specifically for the scanner to use.

Non-authenticated scans may be considered safer because the scanner does not log onto the asset, but the scan coverage can be less comprehensive as a result.

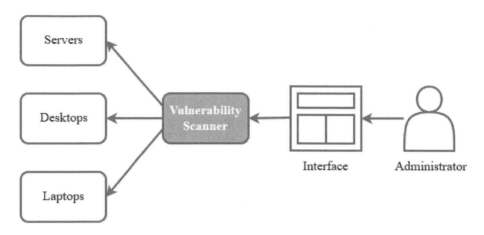

Figure 2.7: An administrator can schedule and launch vulnerability scans against any device on the network, or against segments on the network.

Initiating scans can be trivial but establishing and following a process where findings are followed up with the appropriate groups to ensure systems are patched in a timely manner is a non-trivial effort. Vulnerability scanning can help ensure that endpoints are secured, and all networked assets are identified. For vulnerability scans to be truly effective, however, they need to be part of a dedicated vulnerability management program.

Patching may be one of the most effective ways to improve the security posture of an organization. The implementation of an effective vulnerability management program, however, takes well thought out processes, coordination with several teams, and persistence to get the systems updated. Therefore, it is considered a level 2 security objective.

2.4 CYBER INTELLIGENCE

Level 2 - Cyber intelligence is shared information that provides ways to identify attacks, adversaries and malware, and prevent attacks from taking place as a result. There are many sources of intel, both free and paid-for. There are also several communities that exist where members freely share information based on their own experience and research. Finding intel is not the problem. The challenge is finding information of value: actionable intelligence.

Intel also has an expiration date, and usually a short one at that. Once the details about an attack campaign or malware are known, the effectiveness of the attack is severely diminished since people now know how to protect against it. The tactics adapt and change as a result. Intel needs to be received in a timely manner and assigned an expiration date based on when it was received, or at least reduce its value as time goes on. Otherwise if intel is collected ad infinitum with no culling taking place, the use of this information will require more resources to process and use as the collection grows.

It is recommended for the security team to maintain its own cyber intelligence repository. The information it contains can be plugged into detective and protective controls, and a SIEM, but its contents need to be maintained to ensure the intel is current, relevant, and has value. Despite the challenge of being able to both bring in intelligence feeds and integrate them into monitoring and alerting processes, there is a significant amount of value that cyber intel can provide for detecting and preventing attacks. For these reasons, it is considered a level 2 security objective.

The following are some of the different types of cyber intelligence and how they can be used.

2.4.1 INDICATORS OF COMPROMISE (IOC)

An Indicator of Compromise (IOC) is a piece of information that can be used to help identify malware, an attack, or other potentially malicious activity. IOC's (once obtained from a reputable source) can be added to a continuous monitoring solution such as a SIEM so that if there are any matches of IOC's against actual events observed on endpoints or the network, an alert can be thrown.

Some caution when using IOC's from intel feeds, however: not all are created equal. For example, sometimes non-malicious IP addresses and domains get swept up in the information collected from a previous security event. For example, a security incident may involve a Google IP address, because the attack started when someone searched for something on Google, and the search results included a link to malware (because of a search engine optimization (SEO) attack.) If all IOC's were automatically added to a monitoring solution without prior review, then legitimate sites like Google could start triggering alerts, quickly overwhelming the security staff with false positives. Therefore, take all IOC's with a grain of salt, and subject them to some sort of quality control check before use.

2.4.2 DOMAIN NAMES

A domain name is registered by an individual or an organization and is often intended to represent an entity on the Internet, such as microsoft.com is the web presence for Microsoft Corporation. A domain can be thought of as a mailing address, and at that address can be one or more rooms, or hosts. For example: www.microsoft.com is the main web site for Microsoft, whereas update.microsoft.com is a software update site that Microsoft also hosts.

Domain names do not have to be easy to read either. The domain caff5nzmnlb0jyorapa.com may also be legitimate (and is completely made up), but it impossible to know what it represents just by looking at it. This is where the value of cyber intelligence comes in. If an intel feed provided the IOC caff5nzmnlb0jyorapa.com, and the feed is trustworthy, then this domain can be plugged into detective and protective controls. As a result, an alert would be thrown if a device attempted to visit this domain, identifying a potentially-compromised device. Or an internet proxy could block the domain altogether.

There are also top-level domains (TLD), such as .com, .co.kr, .bank, etc. This is appended to the domain name, and represents a high-level categorization or grouping, such as country of origin or content category (.ru for Russia, .org for non-profits, for example.) There may be limited value in setting up monitoring based on TLD's, however, as blocking an entire category of anything runs the risk of blocking legitimate sites.

2.4.2.1 COMMAND AND CONTROL (C&C) SERVERS

A Command and Control (C&C) server is used by malware to receive instructions, download additional functionality, or receive stolen data. The C&C server can be identified by a domain name or an IP address, and this server can either be a host created by an adversary, or a legitimate server that has been compromised. Being aware of any endpoint communicating with a C&C server may indicate the device is infected with malware.

Using IP addresses to identify C&C servers may not be effective, however, as attackers will "throw off the scent" by using disposable IP addresses, or by using services that quickly change the IP address used by domains at regular and short intervals. Lastly, it is also possible for a C&C server to exist somewhere on the organization's network, versus somewhere on the Internet. This is the modus operandi of several malware variants.

Given all these challenges, there is still value in monitoring and blocking traffic to known C&C servers, as it can prevent malware from being fully functional or from exfiltrating sensitive data.

2.4.3 IP ADDRESSES

One of the least effective ways to identify the source of a scan or attack is to use the IP address from which it originates. IP addresses are basically disposable and can be spoofed or routed through proxies to hide the true source. An IP address may even lead to someone who is innocent but has a compromised device. For these reasons, attribution based on the IP address is not reliable.

Being able to ascribe attribution to a part of the world also can be difficult. The South Korean government experienced over 110K cyber-attacks in 5 years, and almost none of those were sourced from a North Korean IP address. [19] Despite their relatively low value, IP addresses may still provide a starting point to create alerts and dashboards. And sometimes miscreants are lazy and forget to hide their IP address, or sometimes they make mistakes. So, IP addresses are not totally without value from an attribution standpoint.

There are some IP addresses that are perpetually compromised or evil and will always be the source of low-grade attacks and scans. These IP addresses are low hanging fruit that should be plugged into protection controls to block what should otherwise be considered Internet noise.

2.4.4 FILE HASHES

Installing and using hashes with a file integrity checker (FIC) was discussed in section 1 of this book. Known bad file hashes can be supplied by cyber intelligence sources and fed to an alerting solution, such as a SIEM, or perhaps to endpoint FICs themselves. If any files are discovered to have a hash that matches an intel-provided hash, there are several response options, which include generating an alert, and having the endpoint software quarantine the suspicious file.

2.4.5 EMAIL

Phishing is one of the most effective methods used by adversaries to get a victim to download and install malware. Information collected from previous phishing campaigns can provide indicators that can be used to block the same phish from reaching other people's inboxes. The following are elements of an email message that can be used to cross reference IOC's and block malicious emails.

Element	Description
Sender Address	This includes not just what the email client displays, but also the email address that the message was really sent from.
Subject Line	This is the subject of the email message, which is a popular way to identify phishing emails.
Attachments	Files attached to the email (PDF and Office documents, for example) that can be detached and scanned by an appliance such as an email gateway or malware prevention solution (MPS). These attachments can be identified by the file name or checksum.
Sender IP	This is the IP address from which the email originated. This is helpful for identifying email from malicious actors when the sender address is spoofed.
Links in Message Body	The links in an email message can be isolated and evaluated by appliances like an email gateway or analysis sandbox to determine whether the link points to a malicious URL.

Table 2.2: Emails have several identifying properties that can be used to mitigate phishing attacks.

2.5 SUMMARY

Hopefully this section has provided the reader with a good overview of what goes into building out a capability to detect and protect against different types of attacks. Mitigation involves the use of a combination of detective and protection controls placed at strategic locations throughout the network, and at the Internet-facing perimeter. Taking the time to create a comprehensive inventory of all the assets on the network will help ensure that vulnerability scans are thorough, and the security team can quickly get detailed information about any asset that requires investigation or removal from the network. Lastly, the use of cyber intelligence can provide information about adversaries and the attacks they launch, though this information can have varying quality and a limited shelf life.

The maturity level assigned to each item represents the level of maturity an organization's security team (or SOC) should be at to effectively implement the respective security control. It is recommended to pursue these security controls according to what is appropriate for the organization, and in the order of their maturity levels. The order of the items for each level does not represent their importance or the order in which they should be pursued.

2.5.1 LEVEL 1

The following are fundamental security controls, making them level 1 security objectives:

- Alerts
- Reporting

2.5.2 LEVEL 2

The following should be implemented only after a solid security foundation has been established, making them level 2 security objectives:

- SIEM
- Data Loss Prevention
- Vulnerability Scanning
- Cyber Intelligence

2.5.3 LEVEL 3

The following require experienced security staff and adequate resources to implement and operate, making them level 3 security objectives:

- DNS Query Monitoring
- Anonymizer Network Monitoring
- Honeypots

2.6 TERMS AND DEFINITIONS

The following are the terms that were discussed in this section.

Term	Definition
API	Application Programmer Interface. An alternate way to interact with a system.
APT	Advanced Persistent Threat. Definitions vary, but generally an APT is a focused effort to get a persistent and undetectable foothold on a network for purposes such as long-term monitoring and data exfiltration.
Asset Scan	Scanning individual endpoints to identify vulnerabilities, missing patches, and information

	disclosed by the target.
Cyber Intelligence	Shared information about attacks and threat actors that can help protect others against the same threats.
C&C	Command and Control. These are hosts under an attacker's control that provide malware with instructions, modules, payloads, and also receive data exfiltrated by malware.
DDoS	Distributed Denial of Service. A type of network- based attack where a collection of Internet-connected devices overwhelms a specific target such as a web site or gaming network.
DLP	Data Loss Prevention. This is an effort initiated by many organizations to prevent or at least limit the sensitive data that is exfiltrated by employees and insider threats.
DNS	Domain Name Service. Part of the backbone of the Internet, this uses servers across the globe to resolve domain names to IP addresses.
Domain Name	A web server address usually expressed in alpha numeric characters that is often more user friendly than its IP address equivalent.
IOC	Indicator of Compromise. Cyber intelligence collected from security events and incidents that is shared, so that other organizations can use the information to prevent themselves from suffering the same attack.
IPS	Intrusion Prevention System. A security appliance that generates alerts or blocks network packets based on observing certain patterns or behaviors.
Misdirection	A tactic used by adversaries to distract from the actual, main attack.
Network Scan	Scanning the network to identify assets installed on it.
NTP	Network Time Protocol. This is a standard method for getting the time from a centralized clock so that all the devices are synchronized.
SEO	Search Engine Optimization. A type of attack where the miscreant manipulates a search engine so that search results for certain keywords link to sites under the attacker's control.
SIEM	Security Information Event Management. A solution

	that provides a centralized log repository, data mining, alerting, and a consolidated view of events from disparate sources.
TLD	Top Level Domain. Part of a domain that indicates the country of origin or category of a web site.
TOR	The Onion Router. An anonymizer network that allows users to hide their identity on the Internet.
TTP	Tactics Techniques and Procedures. Borrowed from the military, this describes the elements used by an adversary to conduct an attack.

SECTION THREE: RESPOND

What happens is not as important as how you react to what happens."

Ellen Glasgow

I t's not a matter of "if" but "when" a security incident will hit. It is just a matter of time. Even if an entity has been lucky enough not to experience a significant security incident to-date, the appropriate stance to take is that it will happen at some point. This perspective can help ensure preparations are in place.

Of an alert, an event and an incident, it is an incident that is the most severe kind of information security issue. The following are the different types of security issues, in order of severity:

- Alert
- Event
- Incident

Every day there are hundreds to thousands of alerts generated by various security sensors. The priority of the alert, and the analysis performed on it, determines which of these alerts should be considered security events. Resource limitations prevent treating every alert as an event. Alerts should therefore be tuned so that the number of events a team responds to on a typical day does not exceed their capacity to do so.

There will be some events that are severe enough that they are escalated to incident status. This should not be done lightly, as a typical security incident requires the focus of the entire team to stop the damage and bring systems back to the pre-incident state (which can take several hours or even days.) Declaring an incident should involve getting prior approval from leadership and having a response plan available to effectively and efficiently address the issue.

This section covers what goes into the response and remediation of security events and incidents. If a security team operates under the assumption that a serious security incident will eventually take place, then that team will make sure it is prepared. Operating under the belief that the organization is immune to attack (or worse, that everything is 100% secure) provides only a false sense of security and is a setup for certain failure.

Maturity levels are not included in this section.

3.1 EVENT HANDLING

Only a small percentage of security events get escalated to security incidents. Most events can be handled by an individual security analyst, versus requiring an entire team to respond. There is a wide variety of security events that a typical organization will face on a regular basis. The following is a list of just some of those events, with the source that generates the alert, and an example event that caused it.

Source of Alert(s)	Event
Data Loss Prevention (DLP)	An employee emailed a PowerPoint presentation to someone outside of the organization.
Intrusion Prevention System (IPS)	Network activity was observed that matches the signature of a known attack.
Virtual Private Network (VPN) Concentrator	An employee created a VPN tunnel from a location where the organization has no employees.
Wireless Access Point (AP)	An unregistered device was detected in the vicinity of a wireless access point (AP).
Host Based Anti-Virus (AV)	A file was downloaded that was identified as malicious and quarantined as a result.
Malware Prevention System (MPS)	An email sent to an officer of the company had an attachment that was analyzed. The attachment was determined to have a malicious payload.
Firewall	Scans were observed from an IP address registered to a country in Asia.
Proxy	An employee was blocked from accessing a web site that is categorized as gambling.
Web Application Firewall (WAF)	A request to the organization's web site was observed that contained Unicode characters in the request string.

Table 3.1: There are many possible security events that an organization can experience in a typical day.

Sometimes there will be a burst of several to thousands of events within a very short period. Internet-based scans are an example, which happen all the time. Much of it is just the background noise of the Internet and can generate a lot of alerts quickly. A lot of these types of alerts are never elevated to an event that needs to be handled. Sensors can be tuned to filter out or suppress low-severity alerts so that they don't turn into security events that distract from more important higher-severity issues. Events can also be triggered based on the volume of certain alerts, as it could indicate a coordinated attack.

A playbook should be used to provide instructions on how to handle a security event. There will be several different playbooks, as there will be several different kinds of events a team will encounter. Part of the response to an event is to determine whether it is indeed noise that should be suppressed to prevent similar events from being generated in the future. As attack methods constantly change and evolve, the security team should also constantly review its playbooks to ensure they continue to be relevant and effective.

3.1.1 USE CASES

A security team may be approached by other individuals and business units, asking for them to provide security monitoring, such as for a new application or system they are bringing on-line. This request could be driven by regulatory requirements that need to be met. Simply requesting that Security "provide security monitoring" is an inadequate request, however. This is known as "throwing it over the fence." The security team probably knows very little about the new system or software, and how to respond to many of the alerts it generates. In other words, it is not as simple as just saying "here, monitor this."

Often, the security team is not the subject matter expert (SME) of systems and apps that live outside of security. To bridge this knowledge gap, included with the "hand off" should be use cases that are provided by the asset owner and/or SME. Each use case is a document for each alert the system may generate and the corresponding response that should be taken. For example: "If you see alert x, do the following..." Table 3.2 is an example use case document.

Request ID	Acc001
Date of request	11/03/2015
Requesting individual/unit	Accounting
Systems affected	Ledger system
Alert or event	If a user creates invoice, then attempts to pay the same invoice, this is a conflict of interest. An alert should be generated and received by the security operations center.
Request response to be taken	Security should contact the manager of Accounting team. If the manager is not available, then the V.P. of Accounting should be notified.
Requesting individual/unit signature	Eric Delarosa, V.P. of Accounting
Security team acceptance signature and date	David Thompson, Manager of the Security Operations Center

Table 3.2: Use Cases should be documented using a standard form to ensure all required information is collected. This helps ensure that adequate monitoring is provided for the customer.

To effectively monitor a system, Security needs to know "what bad looks like," and members of the security team are often not the best ones to determine this. There are general security best practices (of course) that apply to any IT system, but for any application-specific monitoring, the app owners and SME's need to define alerts and their corresponding responses.

3.1.2 SUPPORT TICKETS

For a team of security analysts that are handling several to hundreds of events daily, communication and documentation are essential. This prevents the duplication of work, reduces confusion, and helps ensure that events are responded to in a correct, timely and consistent manner. Use of a formal ticketing system can facilitate documentation that can be consulted by other team members. This is just a partial list of what ticket handling documentation can provide:

- Educational material for other analysts to learn how to handle future events
- Materials to support the further investigation of events (documentation needs to be retained for an amount of time that is defined by the team and/or organization)
- Support for the research and correlation of other security events and incidents
- The ability to identify commonalities across multiple events

The ticketing system already used by the organization should be leveraged if possible. There is a caveat to this however. Given that the content of these security tickets should be considered confidential (as it could provide information valuable to an attacker) this data should physically reside in a location that is secured with controls that ensure least privilege, confidentiality, and data integrity. For example, the tickets could be stored in a repository database that resides on a network segment that is protected a separate firewall.

Ticket ID	Sec103
Date of Event	11/17/2015
Description	Trudy Joplin made a VPN connection from Athens, Greece at 12/29/2015 05:11 AM.
Resolution	Contacted Trudy's manager who confirmed Trudy is out of the country on vacation until 01/03/2016.
Handled By	Alice Leigh

Table 3.3: Support tickets provide useful information that can reduce data and work duplication.

Per the example in Table 3.3, by having the out of country VPN connection handled once and documented, the next time Trudy "dials in", the analyst handing the alert can quickly see that it has already been investigated and resolved.

3.2 INCIDENT RESPONSE

Security incidents are thankfully rare, as compared to alerts and events. An organization will experience many different types of security events of varying severity on a daily basis. On the rare occasion an event will be determined to be severe enough to be classified as an incident. When that happens, an Incident Response Plan (IRP) should be used. Criteria should be defined in advance to determine whether the event should be treated as an incident.

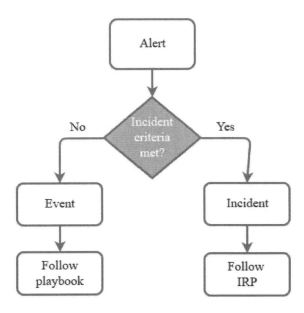

Figure 3.1: An alert must meet certain criteria to be elevated to an incident. Otherwise it should be treated as an event.

How an organization defines security incidents versus events should be determined well before an IRP is used. The definition of what constitutes an incident should be clear and based on quantifiable and objective criteria. Once defined, the next step is to create the corresponding incident response plans. After the plans have been created, they need to be made readily available to those who will be executing them. The confidentiality of the plan should also be enforced (following the rule of least privilege) so that access to the IRPs are restricted to only those who have a "need to know."

Once created, the IRPs should be reviewed on a regular basis. The best method of identifying flaws or improvement opportunities with an IRP is to review and exercise the plan. It is possible that a review will conclude that a plan is no longer relevant or necessary, at which point it can be retired and removed from the IRP repository.

The following section discusses what goes into the creation and maintenance of an effective incident response plan.

3.2.1 INCIDENT RESPONSE PLAN (IRP)

An IRP should be developed well in advance of an actual incident. The worst time to develop a plan is at the time it is needed. To help decide which incidents to prepare for, choose from attacks that your organization is most at risk for. News coverage of past incidents suffered by other organizations can also help identify scenarios to prepare for.

There are several elements that go into an effective IRP. These include the roles played by different members of the response team, the proper way to communicate updates about the incident as it is handled, and the resources that need to be immediately available to facilitate a quick response. The following discusses these elements in more detail.

3.2.1.1 ROLES

Everyone on an Incident Response Team (IRT) should serve a specific function. Sometimes resource constraints cause an individual to serve more than one role. Either way, these are the functions that are provided by a well-defined IRT.

Role	Description
Coordinator	The coordinator serves as the leader of the incident response team. As a conductor is to an orchestra, an IRT coordinator ensures that team members are fulfilling their roles, that the rhythm of the response is maintained, and that progress continues to move forward. The coordinator also ensures and that the team has the resources (technical and otherwise)

	needed for the duration of the response. The person serving this role needs to be able to pivot and perform quick thinking, as the incident response process may change directions several times until resolution.
Scribe	The scribe of the team is responsible for documenting everything that takes place throughout the incident response. The form of the documentation can be an electronic document used for later review, or a PowerPoint presentation slide displayed on a large screen for the entire team to view for updates. The documentation captured should be preserved for after-action analysis (to see what could be done better in the future) as well as potentially support investigations by law enforcement and/or the human resources (HR) department.
Communicator	This person oversees delivering updates throughout the incident response process. There are different kinds of people that require updates and information, such as the operations teams, leadership, executives, and customer support teams. The messages that are delivered need to be tailored to their respective audiences. Defining them, knowing what they need, and being aware of how to effectively communicate with them will serve the communicator well at the time of an actual incident. For smaller teams, the coordinator can also serve as the communicator.
Analyst(s)	There can be several analysts on an incident response team, each focused on a different aspect of handling the incident. Focus areas can include malware analysis, root cause analysis (RCA), intelligence gathering, and identifying how to return operations to the pre-incident state. Analysis may also provide curative actions, such as deploying new AV signatures or creating scripts to remove malware from endpoints. The actions taken should be under the direction of the coordinator so as not to conflict with policy, destroy evidence, or ironically cause more damage as a result.

Table 3.4: There are several different roles that make up an effective incident response team.

3.2.1.2 COMMUNICATION

A communication tree is a list of individuals who should be notified and kept in the loop whenever an incident takes place. This is more than just a simple list of individuals to send emails to, however.

The message needs to be tailored to the recipient. For example, leadership will probably not want to be aware of the technical minutia that goes into root cause analysis (RCA). And not all the security analysts need to be aware of the updates that leadership is providing to the board of directors.

In addition to contact information for individuals, a well-defined communication tree will include the different types of information that should be communicated, and who the appropriate audience is for each. Finally, the messages should be consistent, understandable and relevant to whomever is receiving the update and status messages.

3.2.1.3 RESOURCES

A team will need certain non-personnel resources available in order to respond to an incident and will need them at the start of the response. Key resources include the computers needs to perform the work. These may be the same equipment that is uses for day-to-day operations (e.g. desktop computers), or, if there is a war room (a location dedicated to responding to security incidents), the equipment there needs to be operational and ready to use. The following is a list of equipment that typically should be provided to all responders:

- Desktop or laptop PCs
- Operating systems and applications with current patches and updates
- Network connectivity
- Phone
- Chat/instant messaging
- Access to the latest information about the incident, such as viewing a centrally displayed dashboard that the entire team can view to get updates

Regarding network connectivity, it is preferable to have access to an Internet connection that is not connected to the organization's network. This network connection should also ensure non-attribution, as it will be used to perform research and intelligence gathering. It should be assumed that when an incident takes place, the adversary is monitoring the response in some fashion, such as watching for connection requests from the target to IP addresses owned by attacker, for example. Using a non-attributable Internet connection avoids providing useful information to the adversary who may be watching. Therefore, incident response analysts should have access to a device that is on the internal network in order to use the internal email, chat and other resources. In addition, responders should also have access to a separate Internet connection that is not associated with the production network.

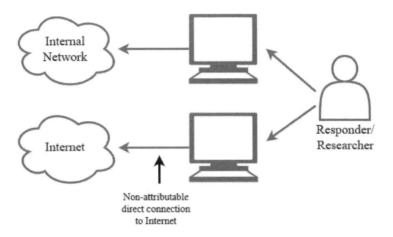

Figure 3.2: At least one response PC needs a non-attributable Internet connection for researching the attack and the attacker.

These resources should be tested periodically to ensure they are ready at the time they are needed. A response should not be delayed because a computer is not working correctly, or because network changes are needed to provide the correct connectivity.

3.2.2 DATA PRESERVATION

It should be assumed that the data collected from an incident will be requested later by law enforcement to support a legal investigation. The data collected from the incident may need to be used as evidence that something did or did not occur, or that someone (or a larger entity like an organization or nation state) is or is not responsible for a criminal act.

For data to be admissible as evidence, it must be credible. The integrity of the data needs to stand up to scrutiny. There should no doubt about whether the data has been tampered with since its creation. Even a reasonable doubt, such as the data owner cannot prove the integrity was maintained throughout the chain of custody, could make the data inadmissible.

Therefore, a data handling process should be defined and followed to support this requirement. Documentation surrounding any data movement, from the time the data was created, should be used. The handling of the documentation also needs to follow a strict protocol to ensure its authenticity and integrity are beyond reproach.

ID	E005
Data Description	Log files from HR database
Documented By	Bruce Shaffer
Filename(s)	hr_11172015_1.log hr_11172015_2.log hr_11172015_3.log
Created	12/17/2015 0600 GMT to 12/17/2015 1300 GMT
Details on Storage	Copied from server hrmong003 and burned to DVD on 12/17/2015 1530 by Bruce Shaffer. Used SFTP to transfer files from server to desktop (secwin42).

Table 3.5: Data artifacts should be documented to ensure their integrity is without doubt. A data tracking form can be used for this purpose.

Forensic analysis may also need to be performed on the devices that were involved in the incident. In that case, these devices should also be treated as future evidence, and so a formal process should be defined and used to do the following:

- Safely remove device from the network
- Capture a snapshot of the memory and processes that are running
- Take an image of the hard drive before the malware can cover its tracks or otherwise destroy the ability to perform a forensic analysis of the device

Some variants of malware exist only in memory, so both a memory and hard drive capture is recommended. Forensic analysis is out of scope for this book but be aware of the data preservation and retention policy for your organization to ensure that it is enforced by the incident response plan and process.

3.2.3 TABLE TOP EXERCISES

A plan has little value if it has not been rehearsed. Running through an IRP, ahead of responding to an actual incident, provides several benefits. First, it validates the plan itself, making sure it is current, relevant, and accurate. Next, it provides practice to the team who will be executing the plan when an incident takes place. Finally, it provides the opportunity to identify areas of improvement and to adapt to an ever-changing threat environment. Every time a plan is exercised will yield improvement opportunities, thereby improving the quality of the plan.

A tabletop exercise is a scheduled meeting with the security team where a scenario is presented. This scenario is prepared ahead of time, needs to be realistic and should challenge the team to determine the best way to respond. Real-world events can provide great inspiration for developing a fictional scenario. As the team works through the exercise, someone should be taking notes, as what is documented may end up in the final incident response plan.

3.2.4 LESSONS LEARNED

One of the most important phases of incident response is the after-action review. Once the dust has settled and operations have been restored to the pre-incident state, a meeting should be set up with the team to review the notes taken by the scribe. This is a great opportunity to go over the incident and identify changes that can be made to improve the IRP. Once updates to the plan have been made, they should be added to a centralized document repository that the entire team (and few others) can access and run through it again in a future tabletop exercise.

3.3 CHANGE MANAGEMENT

Change is inevitable. This is especially true of software and IT systems. Changes are necessary for a variety of reasons, including:

- Adding features
- Removing functionality

- Fixing bugs
- Installing patches
- Applying updates
- Mitigating vulnerabilities

Something that cannot be changed should not be on the production network. This is because there is always a chance that a security vulnerability or other problem will be found. And when it is, it needs to be updated as quickly as possible (ideally before it is exploited.)

When a change is performed, it should be done in a controlled manner that minimizes the chance that something else will break as a result. There are plenty of examples of software patches, intending to fix something, actually ended up breaking something.

To minimize the risk of something going wrong, and being able to quickly recover if it does, a formal change management process should be followed. There are several frameworks available, such as:

- Capability Maturity Model Integration (CMMI)
- National Institute of Standards and Technology (NIST)
- Information Technology Infrastructure Library (ITIL)

Taking the time to integrate a formal change management process, or at least borrow some best practices from established frameworks, will pay dividends in terms of stability, security, and less rework (such as having to back out changes.)

3.4 SUMMARY

Very few security alerts turn into incidents. The majority will be treated as events, and so need to be handled accordingly with the use of playbooks. For incidents, the ability to properly and efficiently respond requires an incident response plan that is rehearsed and reviewed on a periodic basis. There will be more than one plan to cover different scenarios. How a team responds to a data exfiltration incident is going to be different from how DDoS attack is responded to.

The roles the team members serve, the communications tree to be used, and a list of the resources required are all part of a good IRP. Team members should be prepared to serve their required roles, the communications plan should be reviewed and updated, and the required resources should be ready to use and have the connectivity required at the time of the incident. The worst time to discover that something is missing or misconfigured is at the time incident response starts.

Execution of the plan should be done with the assumption that legal proceedings will be part of the aftermath. All data—log files, documentation, images of memory and data storage devices—should be treated as if they will be evidence in a future legal proceeding such as an investigation by law enforcement. Data handling requirements should be included in the plan, and all team members should be made aware and reminded at the time of the incident. The data retention policy of the organization should also inform the procedures to be used for the preservations of artifacts involved in an incident response.

An incident is a great learning opportunity. After-action results should be reviewed by the team to identify what went right, and what can be improved. Performing a "lessons learned" exercise is an important part of a successful IRP. This allows the team to improve the plan for next time (and it should always be assumed that there will be a next time.) Some IRPs may never be used, but when they are, the team and the organization will be thankful for the proactive work that was done to prepare for it.

3.5 TERMS AND DEFINITIONS

The following are the terms that were discussed in this section.

Term	Description
After Action Review	Meeting with the team to discuss how an incident or event was handled. This provides an opportunity to identify what worked well, what could be improved, and to update documentation, playbooks and plans.
Chain of Custody	Strict protocol that is followed to ensure that the integrity of evidence and all related documentation from creation to final delivery.
IRP	Incident Response Plan. This is the plan used by the incident response team to respond to an incident. This plan should be prepared ahead of time and exercised periodically.
IRT	Incident Response Team. This is the group of individuals tasked with being on the front line for

	responding to security incidents in support of protecting the organization from attack.
Playbook	Documented procedure to be used for handling security events.
Pre-Incident State	The environment as it was before a security incident started.
RCA	Root Cause Analysis. This is an analysis process used to determine the origin of an event or incident.
SFTP	Secure File Transfer Protocol. A method of transferring files that is more secure than the legacy File Transfer Protocol.
SME	Subject Matter Expert. An individual who is most knowledgeable about a system, software or process.
War Room	A location dedicated to responding to security incidents.

SECTION FOUR: WRAPPING UP

"When good people in any country cease their vigilance and struggle, then evil men prevail."

Pearl S. Buck

Though it might seem complicated at times, a solid InfoSec foundation can actually be built by implementing well-known security best practices. These can be broken down into individual controls and processes which are implemented in a phased approach. As they are used, the three tenets of information security will be served: protect, detect and respond. If best practices are focused on and implemented effectively, an organization's exposure to attack can be significantly reduced.

At an Enterprise Security web cast on November 2015, Microsoft CEO Satya Nadella summed up the challenge well: "The core hygiene, which we sometimes take for granted, is so important. Because once you start with the operational security posture, you recognize that often, most of the issues have to deal with the lack of patching and the lack of strong credentials. And it's so important for us to not only improve the technology but the security posture you have around the basics." [20]

Good information security is about the basics. Establish a sound foundation for each of the following pillars of information security, then continue to improve on them.

4.1 PROTECT

Defenses should be applied both at the endpoints and network to protect against attacks. Adversaries look for the path of least resistance, and for most targets there are plenty of gaping holes and unpatched systems to exploit. If well-known best practices are applied, and a defense in depth approach is followed, then an entity will be protected against most attacks. Part of a successful protection strategy is to make the job of attacking the organization more work than what the adversary can gain. If you and someone else are being chased by a bear, you don't need to outrun the bear, you only have to outrun that other person. In this analogy, the "other person" are other organizations, and we should have an idea of what represents the bear.

4.2 DETECT

The scary truth is that there is probably malicious activity going on right now on your network; you just haven't found it yet. This is what happened in the infamous attack on Target Stores that cost over $35 million in damages and a few people's jobs. In this case, Target had employed cutting edge security solutions, but the alerts from the device were never observed. [15]

Implementing detective controls involves more than installing sensors that generate alerts. Sensors need to be integrated with existing processes and solutions, such as a centralized SIEM and ticketing solution, to receive and process these alerts. An established process for responding to issues, and ensuring that the sensors themselves are working, are all part of a well-rounded implementation of information security monitoring. As a result, if malicious activity is found, alerts will be generated, and those alerts will be received and promptly responded to by members of the security team.

4.3 RESPOND

When an alert is generated, the receiving party (e.g. the IT security team or Security Operations Center (SOC)), needs to know how to handle the alert. Sensors can generate an almost infinite number of alerts. Most will be ignored as they are triggered by noise of the Internet (e.g. regular low-level scans). Only a handful of these alerts will be actionable security events that require a response.

The appropriate response to events should be determined ahead of time and documented in a way that it is accessible by all responders. The playbook used should be reviewed periodically to ensure that it continues to provide accurate and relevant information. Reviewing notes taken during the response process is a great way to ensure that a playbook is still effective.

On the rare occasion, a security event will be escalated to a security incident. For this to happen, certain criteria need to be met, and possibly a second opinion or formal approval should first be obtained. Declaring an incident is not a trivial move, as a formal incident response plan is followed. Incident response can involve the entire team, as there are several different roles to be served during the response. It should always be considered, however, that a security incident (such as a DDOS attack) may actually be a distraction from a more significant attack that is also taking place against your organization.

Thank you for reading Cyber Security Basics. I hope you find this book useful for your career and/or for studying for a security certification exam. Remember: stay vigilant, trust but verify, and there is no perimeter.

ABOUT THE AUTHOR

Don Franke has worked in information technology for over 20 years. During this time, the roles he served include senior software developer, incident responder, cyber security analyst, and security architect. He has also been a member of several non-profit security organizations and is active in teaching and writing about various topics in cyber security.

His career started before there was a readily-available Internet. One of his first work-related memories is of huddling around a Windows 3.1 PC, struggling to get winsock.dll loaded correctly. This was especially challenging because there was no Internet or Google to search for answers. Once connectivity was established, however, the magical World Wide Web opened, with its random, home-grown sites and blinking text. This was 1994. It was a time when people only cared about sharing information, without much concern about security. How times have changed.

He went on to provide technical support for the analog modems used to connect people to the Internet, and after a couple years started doing web development using Microsoft IIS version 1.0 and Apache httpd with CGI. He continued working as a software engineer, primarily focused on creating web applications and automating data collection from disparate sources. After doing this for several years, the friction he observed between software development and security became strong enough that he decided to deliberately veer his career path to "the dark side": information security.

Don went back to school to get a Master of Science in Information Systems, with an Infrastructure Assurance concentration. He also parlayed that into a couple of well-regarded industry certifications. At work he sought information security projects, and outside of work pursued opportunities to write, teach, and participate in non-profit industry-related organizations.

His latest project is this book. In these pages the author hopes he has captured what has been learned over many years of working in the information security field. The contents are based on his personal experience, and he hopes that it promotes information security education and awareness to those who read it and contributes to the field.

BIBLIOGRAPHY

1. "Fidenae." Wikipedia. 15 April 2015.
<https://en.wikipedia.org/wiki/Fidenae#Stadium_disaster>

2. Gegick, Michael and Barnum, Sean. "Economy of Mechanism." US Department of Homeland Security. 13 September 2005. <https://buildsecurityin.us-cert.gov/articles/knowledge/principles/economy-of-mechanism>

3. Arsenault, Bret. "Enterprise security for our mobile-first, cloud-first world." Microsoft. 17 November 2015.
<http://blogs.microsoft.com/blog/2015/11/17/enterprise-security-for-our-mobile-first-cloud-first-world/>

4. Clapper, James. "Statement for the Record - Worldwide Cyber Threats - House Permanent Select Committee on Intelligence." 10 September 2015.
<https://fas.org/irp/congress/2015_hr/091015clapper.pdf>

5. Fox-Brewster, Thomas. "Netflix Is Dumping Anti-Virus, Presages Death Of An Industry." Forbes.com. 26 August 2015.
<http://www.forbes.com/sites/thomasbrewster/2015/08/26/netflix-and-death-of-anti-virus/>

6. "Morris worm." Wikipedia. 10 October 2015.
<https://en.wikipedia.org/wiki/Morris_worm>

7. Goodin, Dan. "Police body cams found pre-installed with notorious Conficker worm." ArsTechnica.com. 16 November 2015.
<http://arstechnica.com/security/2015/11/police-body-cams-found-pre-installed-with-notorious-conficker-worm/ >

8. Harrison, Virginia. "Nearly 1 million new malware threats released every day." Cnnmoney.com. 14 April 2015.
http://money.cnn.com/2015/04/14/technology/security/cyber-attack-hacks-security/>

9. Keizer, Gregg. "Microsoft urges customers to uninstall 'Blue Screen of Death' update." ComputerWorld. 17 August 2014.
<http://www.computerworld.com/article/2491256/malware-

vulnerabilities/microsoft-urges-customers-to-uninstall-blue-screen-of-death-update.html>

10. Cox, Joseph. "Encryption and Other Tricks Are Making Malvertising Harder to Hunt." Motherboard. 09 December 2015. <http://motherboard.vice.com/read/encryption-and-other-tricks-are-making-malvertising-harder-to-hunt>

11. Mimoso, Michael. "Microsoft Revokes Trust for Certificates Leaked by D-Link." ThreatPost.com. 24 September 2015. <https://threatpost.com/microsoft-revokes-trust-for-certificates-leaked-by-d-link/114804/>

12. Stephenson, Peter. "An unusual and innovative approach to Java security." SC Magazine. 02 March 2015. <http://www.scmagazine.com/an-unusual-and-innovative-approach-to-java-security/article/398234/>

13. "Securing the Human (STH)." SANS. 29 December 2015. <https://securingthehuman.sans.org/>

14. "What's an Advanced Persistent Threat (APT)? A Brief Definition." Damballa. 27 November 2015. <https://www.damballa.com/paper/advanced-persistent-threats-a-brief-description/>

15. Schwartz, Matthew J. "Target Ignored Data Breach Alarms." Dark Reading. 14 March 2014. <http://www.darkreading.com/attacks-and-breaches/target-ignored-data-breach-alarms/d/d-id/1127712>

16. "IPv6." Wikipedia. 12 August 2018. <https://en.wikipedia.org/wiki/IPv6_address>

17. Paul, Kari. "I Bought Adorable Cookies on the Deep Web." Motherboard. December 2015. <http://motherboard.vice.com/read/i-bought-adorable-cookies-on-the-deep-web>

18. Shamah, David. "How honeypot tech tricks hackers into chasing their own tails." ZDNet. November 19, 2015. <http://www.zdnet.com/article/how-super-honeypot-tech-suckers-hackers-into-chasing-their-own-tails/>

19. Iglauer, Philip. "South Korea suffers 110,000 cyberattacks in five years." ZDNet. 15 September 2015. <http://www.zdnet.com/article/south-korea-suffers-110000-cyberattacks-in-five-years/>

20. Nadella, Satya. "Enterprise Security Webcast." Microsoft.com. November 2015. <http://news.microsoft.com/security2015/>

Printed in Great Britain
by Amazon